THE DAY
OF HIS COMING

THE DAY
OF HIS COMING

Prophecies relating
to the time of the end

Peter J. Southgate

First published 2014

Reprinted November 2014

Acknowledgements

All scripture quotations, unless otherwise indicated, are taken from the New King James Version®. Copyright © 1982 by Thomas Nelson. Used by permission. All rights reserved.

Scripture quotations marked (NIV) are taken from the Holy Bible, New International Version®, NIV®. Copyright © 1973, 1978, 1984, 2011 by Biblica, Inc.™ Used by permission of Zondervan. All rights reserved worldwide. www.zondervan.com The "NIV" and "New International Version" are trademarks registered in the United States Patent and Trademark Office by Biblica, Inc.™

Scripture quotations marked (KJV) are taken from The Authorized (King James) Version. Rights in the Authorized Version in the United Kingdom are vested in the Crown. Reproduced by permission of the Crown's patentee, Cambridge University Press.

Scripture quotations marked (RSV) are taken from the Revised Standard Version of the Bible, copyright © 1946, 1952, and 1971 the Division of Christian Education of the National Council of the Churches of Christ in the United States of America. Used by permission. All rights reserved.

ISBN 978-1-874508-53-3

Published by the Dawn Book Supply
5 Station Road, Carlton, Nottingham NG4 3AT, England
Printed and bound in Great Britain

CONTENTS

AUTHOR'S PREFACE

The return of Jesus to earth to establish the Kingdom of God and to reward the faithful is basic Bible teaching and the belief of all true Christians. The Bible gives many signs as to when this event might be expected and how believers can prepare for it. Some of these predictions are quite specific as to timing, others are more general indications, but combined they have given Bible students much encouragement and hope.

With the passage of years many previously expected fulfilments of these predictions have proved premature or incorrect. This can lead to the feeling that even though the coming of Christ is assured, some specific signs of his return are beyond our understanding.

It is hoped that the following pages will encourage a re-examination of the Bible teaching relating to the time of the end. It is not our intention to be dogmatic – for prophecy is not given that we might be prophets ourselves – rather to make suggestions as to how events might transpire, whilst always recognising the fallibility that is common to us all.

With pleasure and appreciation I thank Adrian Pickett for his encouragement and suggestions, Rosalind Wall for her effective proof reading and Emma Perfitt for the design of the cover and the preparation of the text for printing.

It is our earnest prayer that the following will in some small way help to *"make ready a people prepared for the Lord"*, and be to the honour and praise of the Almighty.

P.J.S.

ABBREVIATIONS

JER: Jerusalem Bible

KJV: King James Version

NKJV: New King James Version

LXX: Septuagint Version

NEB: New English Bible

NIV: New International Version

RSV: Revised Standard Version

RV: Revised Version

Chapter 1 The world today

We live in a world that has seen dramatic changes in a very short space of time. In recent years the national, international, social and political climate has altered so radically that the world of thirty years ago seems stable and secure by comparison, and that of the 1950s positively benign.

In any study of the prophecies relating to the time of Christ's return, it would clearly be wrong not to consider the implications of these recent changes. If this event is as near as we hope and believe it to be then we must recognise that the present world situation, rather than that of some decades past, is depicted by the scriptural predictions concerning his coming. There is, of course, always the possibility of sudden changes that will cause the world to revert to situations similar to those of the past, but, as this survey will show, recent changes have been so far-reaching and fundamental that we should not base our expectations on the belief that they will be reversed. If the return of Christ is near then we must take account of the situation as it now is.

Israel

The return of Israel to their ancient homeland after hundreds of years of dispersion is undoubtedly the major general sign that we are living at the time of the end. But, after being successful in three wars against its Arab neighbours, and after having attempted to settle the Palestinian problem by partition, it now finds itself beleaguered. Supported by their Arab neighbours, the Palestinians are making increasing demands, even claiming Jerusalem as their capital city. They support these demands by terrorist activities and suicide bombings that not only have induced terror among the Israelis but have also provoked them to harsh responses that exacerbate rather than control the situation. From the comparative peace following the Camp David agreement in 1978, the situation is now transformed into a reign of terror. It is probably true that it is only the USA's active support for Israel that, humanly speaking, has enabled them to survive.

The Arabs and Islam

The Arab nations surrounding Israel possibly provide another consistent factor in the changing world scene. From before the early days of the establishment of Israel as a separate state, their hostility to the young nation has been consistent and sometimes violent. The practical effects of this antagonism have been made possible by the huge revenues arising from their oil deposits and the virtual stranglehold they have on the industrialised nations in the supply of this resource. But they have to maintain the balance of obtaining maximum revenue from the oil, whilst at the same time keeping on good terms with their customers (who object to the Arab hostility to Israel) and thus ensuring continuing demand. Armed with both Russian and Western weaponry, and outnumbering the Israeli forces many times over, the Arab nations potentially form a ring of steel around that state.

It is extremely significant from a prophetic point of view that the Israeli/Arab problem is now generally recognised as the potential flashpoint for the next world war.

In addition to their hatred of Israel, the other common factor is the Muslim religion, and it is here that recent developments are striking. For the present writer the rapid rise of the influence and power of Islam is something that simply cannot be ignored. After remaining relatively quiescent or localised for centuries, the upsurge of this system as a dominant force in world politics is a feature of only the last few decades. In almost every country new mosques are being built, reflecting the fact that this is the world's fastest growing religion. In a broad band around the eastern hemisphere – from North Africa, through the Middle East, many of the republics to the south of Russia and on to Central and South-east Asia – Islam now predominates. It is also the cause of much tension. In Afghanistan, Pakistan, South Asia, and sub-Saharan Africa the fanaticism of either the Muslim extremists or their religious adversaries has precipitated massacres and civil wars.

Implicit in their thinking is the concept of a "holy war" which they claim the Koran commands to be waged against non-believers or those who allegedly blaspheme their religion. This is particularly directed against the Jews and Israel and their supporters. Martyrdom in such causes, they believe, results in instant admission to paradise. This means that there is no effective sanction or deterrent against the terrorists who invoke this religion as the basis of their actions, as many governments have perforce come to realise.

Terrorism

This naturally leads on to this major development of the past few years. The fanaticism of Islamic extremists (as well as some other groups) has plunged the world into gloom when threatened by *"those things which are coming on the earth"* (Luke 21.26). After a couple of warning shots in the form of bombs at a US embassy in Africa and an attack on one of its warships, the al-Qaeda organisation devastated the world by its simultaneous suicide attacks in New York in September 2001. The failure of the attempts in Afghanistan to exterminate the terrorists means that the Western world, particularly, is still in daily fear of a similar attack, for which there is no really effective protection.

Russia

The last few years have also seen vast changes in the position of Russia. Forty years ago the USSR, with its vast resources of land, armaments and manpower and with its Communist ideology, was regarded as a major threat to world stability. Its annual show of strength in its May Day parades, not to speak of its space programme, emphasised its perceived threat to Western democracy. And this resulted in several stand-offs between the USSR and the Western powers, which buoyed up the hopes of many that the coming of the Lord was near.

But after seventy years, the revolution of 1917 ran out of steam, and the once united power bloc is now a series of separate independent states, all of them experiencing difficulties in the transition from autocratic to democratic rule. Russia has developed a presidential style of government and private enterprise is booming in the upper echelons of its society. Its old antipathy to the West is also reduced, and meetings and sometimes agreements between Russian and Western leaders are occasional features of today's news.

But that said, it seems that Russia has never given up on its territorial expansion. During the transitional period mentioned above some of its associated territory was lost when various regions became independent. In March 2014, despite vociferous opposition from the Western powers, one of these, the Crimean region of Ukraine, was reincorporated into Russia, re-establishing Russian control over the Black Sea port of Sevastapol, thus preserving its access to the Mediterranean. It is also accused of fomenting dissatisfaction in other Russian speaking areas of Europe with a view to bringing them again under the control of the Kremlin But so far it seems that the objective is to achieve its end by intrigue rather than military conquest.

On the religious front, the Orthodox Church, which was banned under the Communist regime, is undergoing revival, with many of the churches reclaimed from secular use to become places of worship once more.

Europe and the European Union

Here is another dramatic change in the past forty or so years that is relevant to the time of the end. From a comparatively loose association of a few European nations has now developed the continent-wide European Union. At the time of writing it has 27 component states, with others expected to join shortly. There is a European Parliament and Commission that sets the rules and standards for its member countries, an integrated financial policy and, for many member states, a single European coinage. There is even talk of political integration, and creating the office of European President, which, if it happens, will mirror the situation from the year 800 when Charlemagne became the undisputed ruler of Europe as head of the Holy Roman Empire.

This leads on to the altered position of the pope. From being a remote figure, rarely seen outside his native country, the office of pontiff has recently entailed worldwide travel to encourage his Catholic followers. This could well have relevance to future events.

As far as the United Kingdom is concerned, the past forty years have seen its continued decline as a major industrial power, and a steady reduction in its armed forces. It is a member of the European Union, but at the same time close-ly associated with the USA, with whom it claims a "special relationship", and tends to support that country in matters of international policy.

The United States of America

With the demise of Communism and the USSR, the USA has become the main superpower in the world, and time will tell what effect this will have. The relaxation of the cold war has resulted in no significant diminution in its arms stockpile, which now contains sophisticated weaponry unimagined a few years ago. And it is quite prepared to use these in unilateral action if it believes its interests are threatened.

But, as the attack on the World Trade Center in 2001 demonstrated, terrorist attacks can be directed at the USA, and robust defence against these is virtually impossible. Much of the Arab/Islamic antipathy to the USA is because of its staunch support for Israel, and should this not be forthcoming for any reason, then Israel's survival would be in doubt, humanly speaking.

Technology

The last few years have also seen a vast change in technology, especially in communication systems. Throughout the world the computer now reigns supreme. Every aspect of public and personal life is now completely dependent on the power inherent in the microchip. Whether it is banking, pensions, transport, telephones, news media, healthcare, food distribution or even the cash register in the local shop, all rely on computing and the electrical supply to energise them. If these systems became inoperative for any reason, then for most of us normal activities would cease, and life itself could be imperilled.

But this ease of communication has another facet. With satellite technology and global cameras, nothing is hidden from view. Local events become world news in an instant, and world response can be as fast. This means that when the final crisis comes, events could develop extremely quickly.

Mass destruction

Until recent times, the ability to produce and control weapons of mass destruction – nuclear warheads, chemical and biological weapons, etc. – was confined to just a few countries, all of them with comparatively stable and responsible governments. But now the possession of such means to annihilate their fellow humans has been extended to smaller and less reliable nations – some of them in the region of the Middle East. The fatal sarin nerve gas attack in the Tokyo subway a few years ago, a similar one in Syria in

2013 and an anthrax infected letter posted in the USA show the potentially lethal effect of such substances getting into the wrong hands.

This, then, is the world to which we expect Christ to return. No doubt there will be minor, perhaps major, variations yet to come but the general picture seems clear. Meanwhile, we have to base our expectations on present realities, not what we have previously thought might happen.

We suggest, therefore, that when we examine the prophecies of the time of the end we must look for their relevance in the world as it is today. It may be that in doing this we will come to some conclusions that are different from those advanced in earlier times, when the world was so different. It may also well be that time will prove some or all of these new conclusions inaccurate – for as we have already stressed, events can change rapidly. But even so, we feel that this approach is better than basing our hopes on possible scenarios that do not reflect the real situation in the present world. We have permanently beside our desk a copy of "Rules for Bible Studies" by Dr. J. Thomas written over 150 years ago, and which we have always tried to follow. Two of these are:

> "Never be afraid of results to which you may be driven by your investigations, as this will inevitably bias your mind and disqualify you to arrive at ultimate truth."

> "Investigate everything you believe – if it is the truth it cannot be injured thereby; if error, the sooner it is corrected the better."

Chapter 2 Peace and safety

We commence our detailed survey of the prophecies concerning the events associated with the return of Christ by looking at the situation described in words found in Thessalonians and Ezekiel. Both seem to suggest that the second coming will be preceded by a period of peace and security. The Thessalonians passage is often taken to predict a general sense of peace in the world, whilst Ezekiel more specifically refers to Israel. We will first look at the Thessalonians reference, here quoted in full:

> *"But concerning the times and the seasons, brethren, you have no need that I should write to you. For you yourselves know perfectly that the day of the Lord so comes as a thief in the night. For when they say, 'Peace and safety!' then sudden destruction comes upon them, as labor pains upon a pregnant woman. And they shall not escape. But you, brethren, are not in darkness, so that this day should overtake you as a thief. You are all sons of light and sons of the day. We are not of the night nor of darkness. Therefore let us not sleep, as others do, but let us watch and be sober. For those who sleep, sleep at night, and those who get drunk are drunk at night. But let us who are of the day be sober, putting on the breastplate of faith and love, and as a helmet the hope of salvation"*
> (I Thessalonians 5.1–8).

When they say, "Peace and safety"

The crucial need here is to identity the "they" who utter the cry of peace and safety. Is Paul referring to the world in general, or to some in the ecclesial world? Or could it be both? Also, does it refer to a specific situation that will develop, or is it a general perception of security? Opinions have been divided, and we will attempt to set out the pros and cons of each.

1. A warning to believers

It has often been remarked that in this passage in Thessalonians the Spirit seems to have directed Paul to Christ's references to his return as contained in the Mount Olivet prophecy. Table 1 clearly demonstrates that Paul's exhortation parallels the words of the Master to his disciples. It has therefore been suggested that inasmuch as the Olivet prophecy was directed to Christ's followers – as was also Paul's letter to the Thessalonians – then the "peace and safety cry" originates from the household of faith rather than from the world at large. In this case Paul is warning the ecclesias to beware of complacency, because the "they" who say "peace and safety" are some brethren and sisters living at the time of the second coming. If this is so, then the exhortation of both Jesus and Paul to stay awake and alert is very relevant to us all.

2. The attitude of the world

Against this view is the strong impression that Paul seems to be contrasting the awareness of the "brethren" (v.4) with the ones who say "peace and safety". "Sudden destruction" (v.3) comes on those who are in darkness (v.4). These terms seem more appropriate to those who do not know the Truth, than to those who know it but are unprepared. Similarly, in the Olivet prophecy the return of Jesus is described as thief-like and a snare to *all those who dwell on the face of the whole earth"* (Luke 21.35), which clearly does not refer to all the saints.

TABLE 1 THE OLIVET PROPHECY AND THESSALONIANS

Olivet prophecy	1 Thessalonians 4–5
"They will see the Son of man coming" (Matthew 24.30; Mark 13.26; Luke 21.27).	*"The Lord himself will descend from heaven"* (4.16).
"He will send his angels..."	*"With the voice of an archangel..."*
"... with a great sound of a trumpet" (Matthew 24.31).	*"... and with the trumpet of God"* (4.16).
"They will gather together his elect" (Matthew 24.31).	*"We* [dead and living]*... shall be caught up"* to *"be with the Lord"* (4.17).
"Until the times of the Gentiles are fulfilled" (Luke 21.24).	*"Concerning the times and the seasons"* (5.1).
"If the master of the house had known in what hour the thief would come" (Matthew 24.43).	*"The day of the Lord so comes as a thief in the night"* (5.2).
"It will come as a snare on all those that dwell on the face of the whole earth" (Luke 21.35).	*"Sudden destruction comes upon them"* (5.3).
"Watch... lest coming suddenly he find you sleeping" (Mark 13.35–36).	*"Let us not sleep, as others do"* (5.6).
"Take heed... lest your hearts be weighed down... with drunkenness" (Luke 21.34; Matthew 24.49).	*"They that get drunk are drunk at night... But let us... be sober"* (5.7–8).
"Virgins, who took their lamps" (Matthew 25.1).	*"You are all the children of light"* (5.5).

The word translated "safety" (*asphaleia*) is also translated "certainty" (Luke 1.4) and comes from a Greek root meaning "unfailing", which is rendered "certain" or "certainly" in several of the places where it occurs in the New Testament. The underlying idea seems to be that of firmness and stability; indeed the RSV translates the phrase as "peace and security". It could be that Paul is describing a world that is stable and not expecting radical change, rather than a world characterised by peace in the conventional sense of the word.

This is possibly confirmed when we find that in using the words "peace and security" Paul is making another allusion to the teaching of the Master in the Olivet prophecy. There, Christ stated (as he frequently did elsewhere) that he will suddenly return to change a world that is apparently stable and continuing: *"For as in the days that were before the flood they were eating and drinking, marrying and giving in marriage, until the day that Noah entered the ark, and did not know until the flood came, and took them all away; so also will the coming of the Son of man be"* (Matthew 24.38–39).

If this interpretation is correct, then neither Paul nor Christ is saying that the second coming will be to a world that is safe and at peace, but rather to one that regards itself as permanent, with no thought of any sudden disruption. This parallels Peter's prediction (where he, too, draws on the analogy of the Flood, as does the Olivet prophecy) that the scoffers of those days will say: *"Where is the promise of his coming. For since the fathers fell asleep, all things continue as they were from the beginning of creation"* (2 Peter 3.4).

3. Specific or general?

Believers often describe Paul's words as "the peace and safety cry", which are taken to describe a specific and widespread exclamation at the anticipation or achievement of peace in a major part of the world. Thus, the various peace conferences and international settlements that have taken place over the years have in their day been viewed as possibly fulfilling this prophecy by advancing the predicted time of peace.

Knowing the fickleness of international politics and, more importantly, aware of the ability of the Almighty to alter events rapidly, we cannot rule out the possibility of world anxiety and conflicts suddenly evaporating. But it is probably being realistic to say that recent history does not give much hope in this direction. The angelic control of world affairs seems to involve gently nudging the nations into God's desired positions rather than causing dramatic changes.

The RSV translates the passage as: *"When people say 'There is peace and security', then sudden destruction will come upon them."* Is it possible that here is almost a proverbial saying setting out a general principle (repeatedly illustrated by history) that peace is almost invariably interrupted by discomfort – in a similar way that in the proverb, pride always goes before a fall? If so, it could be regarded as a general warning against complacency, rather than a prediction of a specific period of peace.

Israel dwelling safely

From general world trends we turn to the specific references to Israel at the time of the end. There are many prophecies that predict the invasion of the restored nation of Israel, and one of these, in Ezekiel 38, describes Israel as dwelling safely at the time of the attack: *"After many days you will be visited. In the latter years you will come into the land of those brought back from the sword and gathered from many people on the mountains of Israel, which had long been desolate; they were brought out of the nations, and now all of them dwell safely"* (v.8); *"You will say, 'I will go up against a land of unwalled villages; I will go to a peaceful people, who dwell safely, all of them dwelling without walls, and having neither bars nor gates'"* (v.11); *"Therefore, son of man, prophesy and say to Gog, 'Thus says the Lord God: "On that day when My people Israel dwell safely, will you not know it?"'"* (v.14).

This thrice-repeated statement that Israel dwells safely at the time of the northern invasion is intensely relevant to any consideration of how these prophecies might be fulfilled; but, as with the "peace and safety cry", there is divergence of views as to what is meant. The "safety" can be taken as literal security, achieved either before or as a result of the return of Christ. Or, as in the Thessalonians passage, the original word could have a different connotation.

1. Safety under Christ's rule

There are several passages that use the original word for "safety" in connection with Israel's security under the rule of the returned Christ. Of the days of Solomon – a clear figure of the reign of David's greater son – we read: *"And Judah and Israel dwelt safely, each man under his vine and under his fig tree, from Dan as far as Beersheba, all the days of Solomon"* (1 Kings 4.25). And, speaking of the Kingdom, Jeremiah says: *"In those days Judah will be saved, and Jerusalem will dwell safely"* (Jeremiah 33.16). Ezekiel frequently uses the same word to describe Israel's future security: *"And they will dwell safely there, build houses, and plant vineyards; yes, they will dwell securely, when I execute judgments upon all those around them who despise them"* (Ezekiel 28.26); *"And they shall be safe in their land... And they shall no longer be a prey for the nations... but they shall dwell safely, and no one shall make them afraid"* (Ezekiel 34.27–28). It is therefore reasonable to conclude that the time of safety described in Ezekiel 38 arises from the protection afforded by Christ on his return to Jerusalem.

In confirmation of this it has been suggested that Ezekiel chapters 36–48 describe a specific sequence of events, in which Israel first is regathered (36–37), then united under the secure rulership of Christ (37.22–28), after which comes the northern invader and his defeat (38–39), and finally the building of the new temple (40–48). Thus, in this model the northern attack on Israel would come after the return of Christ and the establishment of the nucleus of the Kingdom in Jerusalem.

Although this scheme of interpretation appears consistent, some problems arise. First, it seems incongruous that any nation, let alone Israel, under the protection of the all-powerful Christ, would be allowed to experience the severe degradation described in Ezekiel 38–39. Especially as other prophecies which are usually taken as describing the same event, speak of rape, pillage and even captivity (Joel 3, Zechariah 14). Indeed, in the references from Ezekiel quoted above it is explicitly stated that Israel's future safety will not be compromised – *"no more a prey to the heathen"*, *"none shall make them afraid"*.

Further, in Ezekiel 39 (which is often overlooked in such considerations) it is clearly stated that during this period of "safety", Israel was rebellious. Speaking of their future repentance, we read: *"They will forget their shame and all the unfaithfulness they showed towards me when they lived in safety in their land"* (v.26 NIV). The "safety" mentioned here is an obvious reference to that described in chapter 38.8,11,14. Surely Israel will not continue to be unfaithful when they are dwelling safely under the protection of Christ. This would be the reverse of their predicted attitude, as described, for example, in Zechariah 12.9–14.

With regard to the apparently progressive sequence of events in the final chapters of Ezekiel, this is not an uninterrupted sequence. Rather it seems to be a series of distinct (although related) prophecies, each one of which ends with the future blessing of Israel. Thus, chapter 34, after speaking of the return of Israel to their land, culminates in the reign of Christ and the blessings of the Kingdom (vv.23–31); chapter 36 again speaks of the re-populating and increased fertility of the land – and contains clear references to the Kingdom. Then chapter 37 goes back to depict in more detail the regathering of Israel, again concluding with a reference to the installation of their future king. Then comes the northern invasion of chapters 38–39, resulting in Israel's acceptance of the Lord (39.22): something that they presumably had not done before the attack. It could be argued that these concluding sections of Ezekiel are each describing a single aspect of Israel's restoration that leads up to the final outcome, rather than describing sequential events.

2. Safety prior to the Gogian invasion

An alternative view is that Israel as we know it today, despite the current bitter conflicts with its neighbours, will be experiencing safety and peace prior to the northern invasion. This is, of course, a possibility and, if we take the words at their face value, a probability. Although, as we write, the war clouds remain heavy in the area, this scenario would mean that the current problems will be solved by some means and Israel will recover its prosperity and live in peace with its neighbours. This would require dramatic changes in circumstances and attitudes on all sides, but nothing is beyond the power of the Almighty.

3. The meaning of "safety"

The meaning of the Hebrew word translated "safety" must also be brought into this discussion. It is the word *betach* and it is translated as "safety", "safely" or "safe" in the majority of the 42 occasions it occurs in the Old Testament. But there are some occasions where this understanding would obviously be inappropriate, and these may have a bearing on its use in Ezekiel 38–39.

For example, Jeremiah foretold Nebuchadnezzar's attack on Hazor in Galilee, describing a very similar situation to that applying to Israel in the last days: *"Arise, go up to the wealthy nation, that dwells securely [betach], saith the LORD, which have neither gates nor bars, which dwell alone"* (49.31). In view of the impending threat from Babylon here being described – which must have been well known to Hazor – it is understandable that some translators chose "without care" (KJV) or "in confidence" (NIV) rather than "securely" to describe their obviously perilous situation. Indeed "without care" or "care-less" seems to be a basic idea behind the word. Thus, in Ezekiel 39.6 (KJV) Magog is described as dwelling "carelessly" (*betach*), that is, "confidently", but certainly not in safety, as the context shows. In 38.8 the KJV margin also renders "safely" as "confidently".

So, is Ezekiel in chapter 38 saying that at the time of the future invasion Israel will be dwelling confidently, resting on their own military might, rather than suggesting that they will be safe and at peace?

4. Without walls, bars and gates

This describes the nation that will be invaded. Protective walls, with gates that could be barred as a defence against attack, were a common feature of all major cities in the prophet's days, and many attempts have been made to find their equivalents in modern Israel. But do we have to take the words literally? Clearly, if there were no walls, there also would have been no gates or bars needing to secure them, so it is possible that a metaphorical allusion is intended. In Bible times the unwalled towns and villages were virtually defenceless, and they easily succumbed to any assault. Could it therefore be that by using this idiom Ezekiel was simply saying that at the time of the invasion Israel would be very vulnerable to attack?

Final comment

We have tried to outline and comment on the various interpretations that have been put on these two passages as objectively as possible without, we trust, being biased in favour of any one view. Our intention is to let readers make their own judgements. We recognise that there could be a major difference of opinion, especially as to whether the attack by Gog occurs before or after the return of Christ to Israel. Maybe the various options will become clearer as we continue with this absorbing study.

Chapter 3 One attack or two?

Both Old and New Testaments predict that at the time of the end a confederacy of nations will attack God's people prior to the submission of the whole world to Christ and the immortalised saints. The Old Testament prophets describe hordes of nations coming upon Israel and Jerusalem (Ezekiel 38–39; Joel 3; Zechariah 14), from which invasion they are ultimately delivered by divine intervention. In the New Testament the book of Revelation depicts a similar gathering of nations that unsuccessfully attack Christ and the saints (chapters 17 and 19). Are these two sets of prophecies describing the same event, or should we look for more than one conflict between God and man prior to the establishment of the Kingdom? This is what the present chapter will explore, leaving the detailed identification of the assailants for future ones.

A single campaign?

One widely accepted view tends to combine all the prophecies into one event. The Gogian invasion (Ezekiel 38–39) will be defeated by the newly returned Christ, assisted by the immortalised saints, in an open manifestation of the power of God (Revelation 19.11–21) and the Kingdom set up. To accommodate the New Testament prophecies into this scenario it is assumed that the attack on Israel described in such passages as Ezekiel 38–39 will be in collaboration with the papacy and other European powers, represented in Revelation by "Babylon the great", "the beast" and the "false prophet".

Two invasions?

An alternative view is that two attacks are being predicted, with different protagonists and a significant interval between the two battles. This concept sees the first attack being the Gogian invasion, which occurs before the return of Christ to Israel. This invading host is destroyed, by apparently non-miraculous means, after which the nucleus of the Kingdom will be set up in Jerusalem under the rulership of Christ. Later, the series of events depicted in Revelation 14 will occur – including the preaching of the everlasting gospel that invites all nations to accept the new world ruler in Jerusalem (see also Psalm 2.10–12). This offer will be rejected by the papacy and its European allies, who will mount the second attack – a campaign to remove the alleged usurper as described in Revelation 19.

In attempting to decide between these alternatives it is helpful to compare and contrast the relevant features of the two sets of prophecies. This is done in Table 2, which should now be examined before proceeding.

TABLE 2 THE MAIN FEATURES OF THE TWO SETS OF PROPHECIES.

Description	Ezekiel 38–9; Joel 3; Zechariah 14	Revelation 16, 17 and 19
Time of attack	When Israel regathered: Ezekiel 38.8,12; Joel 3.1.	After completion of seven vials: Revelation 17.1; and after the marriage of the Lamb: Revelation 19.1–10.
The attackers	Gog and allies: Ezekiel 38; "All nations": Joel 3.2.	Babylonish harlot, beast, kings of earth: Revelation 17.14;

		influenced by unclean spirits from mouth of dragon, beast and false prophet: Revelation 16.13–14.
Reason for attack	Spoil: Ezekiel 38.12; Joel 3.5; Zechariah 14.1; to defile Zion: Micah 4.11.	War of opposition to Christ: Revelation 19.19; Psalm 2.
The attacked	Nation of Israel, Jerusalem.	Christ and immortalised saints: Revelation 17.14; 19.11–14.
Observers (?) of the attack	Sheba, Dedan and merchants of Tarshish.	
Success of attack	Spoil taken: Ezekiel 39.10; Jerusalem captured: Zechariah 14.2; Israel made captives: Joel 3.6; Zechariah 14.2.	The Lamb overcomes them: Revelation 17.14; Beast, false prophet and worshippers "taken": Revelation 19.20.
Mode of defeat	Pestilence, rain, hailstones, fire, brimstone, earthquake: Ezekiel 38.19–22; plague: Zechariah 14.12. By in-fighting among invaders: Ezekiel 38.21; Zechariah 14.13. Judah fights them: Zechariah 14.14.	Sharp sword of Christ: Revelation 19.15,21.
Place of defeat	Mountains of Israel: Ezekiel 39.4.	Armageddon: Revelation 16.16.
Fate of attackers	Food for ravenous birds and beasts; remains buried in Israel: Ezekiel 39.4,11,17–20.	Food for ravenous birds; remains cast into lake of fire: Revelation 19.20–21.
Result of attack	God sanctified in eyes of Israel and nations: Ezekiel 38.23; 39.22.	

Despite some similarities in the two columns, which could suggest that only one event is being predicted, it can be argued that most of the differences are sufficiently significant to suggest that two separate incursions are being depicted.

Differing features of the invasions

In addition to the difference in the timing and the overall results of the two attacks, the motives for, the initial success and the means of defeat of the invasions are strikingly different. The objective of the Old Testament invader is plunder and defilement, and this is at first successful. The New Testament campaign is specifically against Christ and the saints, apparently with immediate failure. Further, the means of defeat are different, and this is often not appreciated. Ezekiel is very specific that the Gogian invasion is destroyed by what could be seen as non-miraculous means. Natural disasters, in-fighting among the protagonists, and a counter-attack by Israel are all involved in the divinely controlled defeat of the invader. But the New Testament attack is depicted as a deliberate challenge to the authority of Christ, which will be met by an open manifestation of divine power and authority.

It could be that this difference is significant. If the defeat of Gog were to be seen by the world as a clear example of open divine power and the absolute superiority of the returned Christ, it would make less likely any later opposition to this new ruler in Jerusalem. But if the events of the first invasion could be seen by the world as an unfortunate combination of natural disasters (and sinful man would want to believe such a view rather than accept the claims of Christ, maybe even thinking that the Israelis have found some new technology to annihilate their enemies), then it would be more likely to refuse the request for submission to the returned Jesus as demanded by the later edict to: *"fear God and give glory to him, for the hour of his judgment is come"* (Revelation 14.7).

Present situation

The present-day implications for the two alternatives are considerable. If the "single attack" suggestion were correct, it would involve collaboration between very many disparate groups in the attack on Israel. All the nations mentioned in Ezekiel 38–9, plus the "beast" nations of Europe (taking our usually accepted understanding of that symbol), together with the influence of "Babylon", the Roman Catholic church, will in some way have to unite in a campaign of plunder against Israel. In the present political situation it is difficult to see the motive or probability of such a union.

The "two attack" scenario would certainly seem to fit more comfortably. Without, at this stage, attempting to identify the protagonists involved (reserved for a later chapter), the current Middle East turmoil, which is directed at settling old scores with Israel, readily lends itself to a fulfilment of at least some of the Old Testament prophecies. On the other hand, the gradual unification of Europe and the continuing influence of the papacy would seem to suggest that the New Testament predictions of direct opposition to the returned Christ later on from this quarter might be more appropriate and likely.

Having said this, we must not rule out the possibility that world situations can dramatically and rapidly change, and we would be wise not to fix our expectations on any one interpretation of prophetic details. Certainly there are passages and arguments that can be used in support of both possible outcomes. In one sense the details are unimportant to Christian life now. We can take comfort that the general picture is clear – the return of Jesus will be at a time when the "nations are angry, and God's wrath is come", with the result that God's king will be firmly set on His holy hill of Zion. The important question, about which there can be no debate, is: are we ready?

Chapter 4 The northern invader

We now look in more detail at the nations that are depicted in the Old Testament as attacking the restored nation of Israel. The main account, of course, is in Ezekiel 38–39, but we must not ignore other passages. Nor must we let any familiarity with Ezekiel's description make us gloss over some of its features.

Gog

The first thing to note is that the invasion will be under the leadership of a man styled "Gog". He will evidently be a powerful and charismatic leader, for he will be able to assemble a great company of diverse peoples for his attack upon Israel. A king of the Amalekites had a similar name, Agag, in the days of Samuel; and Balaam had earlier prophesied that Israel's future king would be higher than Agag (Numbers 24.7). The Septuagint terms this vanquished ruler "Gog". Apart from this possible link there is no other Scripture enabling us to identify this ruler. There is, of course, the possibility that in the prophecy Gog is a figurehead for a nation, just as it was said of Nebuchadnezzar: *"You are this head of gold"*, the Babylonian kingdom being intended.

In attempting to identify the modern equivalents of the nations confederate with Gog, we must always remember that those Ezekiel describes were actual nations existing in his day, the 6th century BC. These were the times of Assyrian and Babylonian control of the Middle East, and some of their writings can throw light on their identification and help us find their modern equivalents.

The land of Magog

Gog is the ruler of Magog. The prefix "ma" or "mai" was often used by ancient nations to indicate a country: thus "Magog" could mean "the land of Gog".

Where is Magog? First, the scriptural information. The name first occurs in Genesis 10 in the list of the descendants of Noah. In fact many of the countries mentioned in Ezekiel are introduced to us here: *"The sons of Japheth were Gomer, Magog, Madai, Javan, Tubal, Meshech, and Tiras. The sons of Gomer were Ashkenaz, r iphath, and Togarmah. The sons of Javan were Elishah, Tarshish, Kittim, and Dodanim. From these the coastland peoples of the Gentiles were separated into their lands, everyone according to his language, according to their families, into their nations"* (vv.2–5).

In commenting on this passage Josephus says of Magog that he "founded those that from him were called *Magogites*, but who are by the Greeks called *Scythians*" (*Antiquities* 1.6.1). The Scythians are well known to history as a warlike, horse-riding nation (cp. Ezekiel 38.15) that inhabited Asia Minor and the Black Sea region in the 6–7th centuries BC, often confronting Assyria and Babylonia. The Assyrians called the Scythians "Saki", and their territory lay between the Black and Caspian Seas, south of the Caucasus Mountains; but by the 3rd century BC had extended into the areas immediately to the north of those seas.

The Scythians of those days had a king whose name was similar to the Hebrew "Gog". The Assyrian king Asshurbanipal conducted a campaign in the north of his realm, in which, according to the clay cylinder recording the event, he captured alive and brought to Nineveh "two sons of Gagi, the chief of the Saki". So there was a literal Gog, a chief prince of the land of Magog existing in the times in which Ezekiel prophesied.

The parallelism in the Hebrew of Ezekiel 39.6 could suggest a country near a coastline: *"And I will send a fire on Magog, and among them that live in security in the coastlands"*. This again would place the Magog of those days in Asia Minor, modern Turkey, making the reference to the sea coast appropriate. In fact the Assyrians received an ambassador from a Lydian king in Asia Minor, called in Assyrian "Gugu", showing that this name was not uncommon in those days. In either case Magog was situated north of Israel.

Meshech and Tubal

These two – often linked together in both Scripture and profane records – are descended from Japheth and are clearly associated with Magog in the prophecy inasmuch as they are ruled by Gog. Their territory is well documented. Josephus describes them as Cappadocians, and they lived between the Caspian and Black Seas. Again, the Babylonians and Assyrians made many references to these peoples under names such as Moschi and Tibareni. In the Assyrian inscriptions they are regularly associated with the terms Mushkii and Tuplai.

They seem to have been sub-divisions of the Scythian tribes that spread across the area north of the Black and Caspian Seas, even extending across to the borders of India.

Some have suggested a link between the names Meshech and Tubal with the cities Moscow and Tobolsk, but neither of these existed in Ezekiel's time. Moscow, the Russian capital, was founded in 1147 and Tobolsk, the Siberian capital, not until 1585, and these names would have been unknown in the 7th century BC.

Prince of Rosh

It is well known that the KJV "chief prince of Meshech and Tubal" can alternatively be translated "prince of Rosh, Meshech and Tubal", thus suggesting another territory under the influence of Gog. This is widely interpreted as a reference to an area covered by modern Russia. Our linguistic limitations prevent an analysis here of the merits of the two alternatives. Comparing the various translations, however, it does seem that the preponderance is in favour of treating the Hebrew rosh as a proper name. In the versions we consulted, three retained the word "chief" in the text (KJV, RSV, NIV); whilst eight (RV, NEB, Young's Literal, Jerusalem Bible, LXX, Darby, Rotherham, Moffatt) translated it as "Rosh". But in many of these, uncertainty is indicated by the margin giving the alternative, "chief prince".

If a tribe or place called Rosh is intended, we must look outside Scripture for its identification, for there is no other Biblical reference to it as a country. Nor does there seem to be any reference to the name in sources outside the Bible at the time of Ezekiel's prophecy. In fact it was not applied to any area to the north of Israel until about 1500 years later. The modern name "Russia" is recognised as being derived from a word similar to the Hebrew *rosh* but, unlike the other names mentioned by Ezekiel, the ancients would have known neither a land or people so described.

The *Encyclopaedia Britannica* says: "The name 'Russia' is derived through *r ossiya* from Slavonic *r us* or *r os*, a name first given to the Scandinavians who founded a principality on the Dnieper in the 9th century. The name *r us* is probably derived from *r uotsi* (a Finnish name for the Swedes) which seems to be a corruption of the Swedish *rothsmenn* 'rowers' or 'seafarers'."

So if the Hebrew *rosh* is a proper noun, and if, unlike the others mentioned, it refers to a country that was not then in existence under that name, then it must be an example of the undoubted power of inspiration to predict things far outside the knowledge of the inspired writers.

"From the north parts"

But what is not in doubt is that the nations so far mentioned as being under the control of Gog are all to the north of Israel, and situated in the area between or adjacent to the Black and Caspian Seas. As Ezekiel says: *"Thou shalt come from thy place out of the north parts, thou, and many people with thee, all of them riding upon horses, a great company, and a mighty army"* (38.15 KJV). The original for "the north parts" means literally "the sides of the north", and is variously translated to indicate the extreme north: "far recesses of the north" (NEB); "the far north" (NIV, JER); "the uttermost parts of the north" (RSV, Darby); and "remote parts of the north" (Rotherham).

It is tempting to say, therefore, that these versions speak of a country or power high in the northern latitudes, but in fact the original word translated "parts" or "sides" does not necessarily seem to be used to indicate distance, but rather to describe any boundary or perimeter of a thing or place. For example, we are told that Jonah went "down into the *sides* of the ship", clearly not a long distance away. So the word could be used in Ezekiel to describe a northern boundary, wherever that happened to be. An example of the more limited use of the term is found in Jeremiah, where the prophet is threatening the Babylonian invasion. We know that Babylon was situated to the north-east of Jerusalem (although because of the intervening desert any invasion would have come from the north), yet from the parallelism so characteristic of Scripture we find that Jeremiah uses the same phrase as Ezekiel: *"Thus saith the LOr D, 'Behold, a people cometh from the north country, and a great nation shall be raised from the sides of the earth'"* (Jeremiah 6.22 KJV). Clearly, in this case "the sides of the earth" does not necessarily mean a very remote distance (see also Psalm 48.2 and Isaiah 14.13).

Persia, Ethiopia and Libya

Returning to the list of the invaders, we find that Ezekiel next mentions these three countries. Immediately we notice a change of direction, for here are nations that encircle Israel on the east and south.

Persia is easily identified as the country east of Babylon, Assyria and the Tigris and Euphrates plain: today it is called Iran.

Ancient Ethiopia is not in exactly the same place as its modern namesake. The Hebrew word is Cush, meaning "black", almost certainly a reference to the dark-skinned descendants of Ham. Many scriptural references link Cush with Egypt (Psalm 68.31; Isaiah 20.4–5; 43.3; 45.14, etc.), and from profane history we know that the term was used of the country of the upper (southern) reaches of the river Nile. Josephus uses it to describe the people of this area, approximately modern Sudan.

But some contend that the races in southern Egypt were a later offshoot of tribes more to the north and east. For example, the geographer Bochart believed that the Cushites originated in Arabia, and only later crossed into Africa. This is confirmed by the nineteenth century archaeologist A.H. Sayce (*The Higher Criticism and the Monuments* p.133, SPCK, 1895). There is some scriptural indication of this in that the other descendants of the Cush mentioned in Genesis 10.6 were in the Arabian region. Moses' wife, a Midianite from the same area, was called a Cushite (Numbers 12.1). Also Habakkuk 3.7 links Cush and Midian at the time of the exodus. But on the assumption that Ezekiel was referring to the situation as it was in his day, the view that it referred to Upper Egypt is probably preferred.

Libya (Heb. *Phut*) has always been associated with the area of North Africa that still bears a similar name. In fact the three countries Libya, Ethiopia and Egypt are linked together in Scripture, probably confirming their geographical association (Daniel 11.43).

Gomer and Togarmah

Again our attention is directed northwards, and the allies in this confederacy are completed with the mention of Gomer and Togarmah (v.6).

Gomer (*Gimirra* in the Assyrian texts) is almost certainly the tribe known to the ancients as the Cimmerians, who lived north of the Black Sea, and have left their linguistic legacy in the area known as "Crimea". Just before the time of Ezekiel they had settled in Asia Minor, hence the reference by Josephus that "Gomer founded those whom the Greeks now call Galatians [Gauls], but were then called *Gomerites*". They gave their name to the area still known in New Testament times as *Galatia*. But about the time of Ezekiel's prophecy they were expelled back to the territory of the Scythians, with whom they were then closely associated.

During the centuries after Ezekiel's time these Gauls, or Cimmerians, spread across Europe, extending even to Wales, where the name persists in the native term for that country: Cymru.

Finally we come to Togarmah, of which little is known apart from some references in Assyrian times which locate it in Armenia. In ancient times this was the region of Ararat, south of the Black Sea.

Having identified the countries and areas spoken of by Ezekiel in his day, in the next chapter we will consider their modern equivalents in an attempt to identify the various components of the invasion predicted by the prophet.

Chapter 5 The modern equivalents of the invading nations

In the previous chapter we identified the areas occupied by the various nations mentioned in Ezekiel 38–39. Those findings are summarised in the map. Also indicated in italic type are the modern nations in that part of the world. To the north of the area covered by the map is the territory now occupied by Russia. But a nation called *r osh*, the precursor of the name *r ussia*, was unknown to Ezekiel, for it was not applied to the region until about 1500 years later.

FIGURE 1   THE NATIONS IN EZEKIEL'S DAY

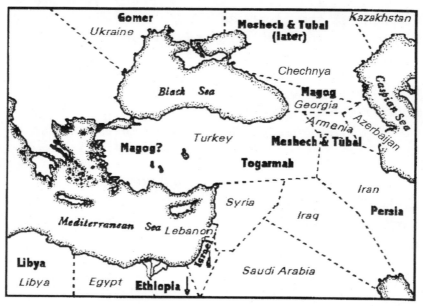

On the assumption that the latter-day equivalents of the nations mentioned by Ezekiel occupy the same territory as the ancient peoples he mentions, it is generally easy to identify Israel's future attackers. It can readily be seen that these come from lands that surround Israel. Some, such as Libya, Ethiopia and Persia, are easily recognised as modern nations. Egypt is not specifically mentioned by Ezekiel, but reference to a concordance will show that frequently Egypt and Ethiopia are closely linked in Scripture (e.g. Isaiah 20.5; 43.3; 45.14; Ezekiel 30.4). But the regions to the north of Israel have undergone recent changes that we should probably take into account.

In the early 1990s several autonomous republics were formed from the USSR, based mainly on existing ethnic divisions, particularly in the southern territory of the previous Soviet Union. Those relevant to our study are Azerbaijan, Georgia, Chechnya, the Ukraine and possibly Kazakhstan. Together with the small country known as Armenia, these occupy the territories known to Ezekiel as Meshech, Tubal, Magog, Togarmah and Gomer.

From the map it will also be seen that Turkey extends to the north of Israel, and to be consistent in our interpretation we must not discount the possibility of that nation's involvement in the co-ordinated attack. As mentioned in the previous chapter there was probably a Magog here in ancient times.

Psalm 83

Many believe that the attack on Israel described in this psalm is the same as that in Ezekiel. The motive is annihilation of Israel: *"They have taken crafty counsel against your people... They have said, 'Come, and let us cut them off from being a nation; that the name of Israel may be remembered no more'"* (vv.3–4). As in Ezekiel, the attack is by a confederacy of nations: *"For they have consulted together with one consent: they form a confederacy against you"* (v.5).

In this prophecy it is the immediate neighbours of Israel that are implicated: *"The tents of Edom, and the Ishmaelites; Moab and the Hagaretes; Gebal, Ammon, and Amalek; Philistia with the inhabitants of Tyre; Assyria has also joined with them; they have helped the children of Lot"* (vv.6–8). The modern equivalents of these nations are Jordan (Edom, Moab, Ammon, etc.), Iraq (Assyria), Lebanon (Tyre) and Gaza (Philistia).

United against Israel

If the above reasoning and identification is correct, then it seems that a co-ordinated attack on present day Israel will be made by virtually all the nations that encircle God's people. And it can be no coincidence that the vast majority of them have a significant Muslim population. The following proportion of Muslims in each country was obtained from *Compton's World Atlas:* Azerbaijan, 93%; Egypt, 94%; Ethiopia, 50%; Iran, 99%; Iraq, 97%; Kazakhstan, 47%; Jordan, 92%; Libya, 97%; Saudi Arabia, 100%; Sudan, 75%; Syria, 90%. Chechnya is potentially an Islamic republic. (The exceptions are Armenia, Georgia and the Ukraine, which are listed as predominately Orthodox Christian.) Whilst the degree of militancy towards Israel varies from state to state, a common factor is that they all regard the presence of Israel as an intrusion into a basically Islamic region.

What will be the trigger for the attack remains to be seen. The continuing tension between Israel and the Palestinians, the perpetual refugee problem and the Arab's claim on Jerusalem as their capital city may each be factors. But in addition, some external situation may develop, of which we are currently unaware, that will induce the confederates to believe that their attack on Israel will be successful.

Gog of the land of Magog

What does seem to be indicated is that one individual, Gog, will mastermind the attack; although the possibility that he represents a figurehead for a nation must not be overlooked. It would seem, therefore, that we could look for an Islamic leader, or nation, that will take the lead in igniting these nations against Israel. And this "chief prince" will come from the ancient land of Magog, that is, the region around the Black and Caspian Seas.

Similarly, the main thrust of the attack will come from the north. But in view of the many confederate nations that will be involved, it would be reasonable to expect that through-out the Middle East considerable troop and equipment movements would precede the attack. Whilst in modern warfare such movements can be made quickly, it does seem to assume that the confederate nations will feel that they have control over the region – hence the earlier suggestion that there may be unforeseen developments.

Rosh

The above analysis has been made on the basis that Ezekiel's Rosh does not refer to a country. But we must not rule out the possibility that the Spirit, with its infinite foreknowledge, inserted among the names then familiar to Ezekiel the name of a then unknown region that fifteen hundred years later would become known as Russia. In this case the leading protagonist in this future attack would be the ruler of the Russian nation, as our conventional interpretation envisages.

In this case there would need to be an incentive for an invasion led by Russia, and a reason for a military alliance with the nations surrounding Israel. Although things may change rapidly, it does seem that neither of these requirements is likely to be met in the near future. Russia is currently concerned with building its industrial base after years of Communist mismanagement and neglect. Its armed forces are inferior to those in the Western world. And, although its seems to have expansionist intentions into its former areas of influence in Europe, any attack on Israel would severely prejudice its political and commercial ties with the West. But, as we say once more, things could suddenly change.

This does not mean that we suggest that Russia has no important role in the events of the time of the end, only that it may not be involved in the initial attack on Israel and Jerusalem.

Chapter 6 The merchants of Tarshish and the young lions

Having considered a possible identity of the latter-day attackers of Israel, it is now appropriate to discuss those who are often considered to be the opponents of these northern invaders.

Those who challenge the sinister motives of Gog and his allies are: *"Sheba, Dedan, the merchants of Tarshish, and all their young lions, who say, 'Have you come to take plunder? Have you gathered your army to take booty, to carry away silver and gold, to take away livestock and goods, to take great plunder?'"* (Ezekiel 38.13).

We now examine the identification and role of Sheba and Dedan, who, with the merchants of Tarshish and the young lions, will apparently challenge Gog and his confederates as they descend on the mountains of Israel as described in Ezekiel chapters 38 and 39.

Earlier suggestions

In the middle of the nineteenth century, students of Scripture and observers of contemporary world events in the light of biblical prophecies identified Great Britain and her numerous colonial allies as the power that would protect the Jews. Great Britain was seen as a pre-eminent promoter of the return of God's scattered people to the land of Palestine, the prelude to the final realisation of the Kingdom of God centred in Israel's homeland.

Several Old Testament prophecies were interpreted as being

of special significance for Britain's role in the latter days. Isaiah 16, a prophecy concerning Moab, was given a specific latter-day meaning: *"Let my outcasts dwell with you, O Moab; be a shelter to them from the face of the spoiler"* (v.4). Here, Great Britain was identified as the latter-day Moab (*Elpis Israel* 13th edn, p.444), where John Thomas identified the British power with several nations mentioned in the Bible. These were Sheba, Dedan, Tarshish and the accompanying young lions, (p.433), Tyre (*Eureka* vol. III p.409), and the Queen of Sheba (p.601; *Exposition of Daniel* p.93). Great Britain was also seen as a close collaborator with Egypt (p.97). With the exception of the identification of Tarshish, most of these interpretations have been revised in the light of twentieth century history, which saw the decline of British power and influence.

Sheba and Dedan

Modern archaeological studies provide little doubt that the biblical kingdom of Sheba was the ancient Saba in Yemen, Southern Arabia. It existed from 1200 BC until AD 275, and Scripture depicts it as a prosperous mercantile nation. In the days of Solomon its queen came to Israel with a vast amount of gold and precious spices, and elsewhere it is mentioned as a rich trading nation (Isaiah 60.6; Ezekiel 27.22). Its rulers, along with those of Tarshish, will offer rich gifts to the latter-day Solomon (Psalm 72.10,15).

Dedan is also clearly identified as being in modern Saudi Arabia, and is now known as Al Ula. This location is confirmed by the reference in Isaiah when he addresses Arabia: *"The burden against Arabia. In the forest in Arabia you will lodge, O you travelling companies of the Dedanites"* (21.13). Dedan, too, was a mercantile area known for its ivory, ebony and horses' saddlecloths (Ezekiel 27.15,20).

The modern equivalents of the ancient Sheba and Dedan are therefore located in the Arabian peninsula.

Tarshish

Quite a few modern students of prophecy believe that Tarshish signifies the present United Kingdom. On this basis there is a view that the United Kingdom needs to be separate from the European Union, and has no role in a future European confederation. Instead the United Kingdom is seen as a partner in the pro-Israeli policies of the United States of America. Recent events relating to Europe have provided some support for this view.

Where was Tarshish?

It is clear from Scripture that there were at least two ancient places with the name Tarshish. One is undoubtedly to the south of the land of Israel. From his Red Sea port on the Gulf of Aqaba Solomon sent merchant ships every three years to countries that supplied such items as gold, silver, ivory, apes and monkeys, goods that clearly originated from areas well south of Israel. So Tarshish was probably somewhere in the Arabian peninsular, or possibly the coast of East Africa or even Sri Lanka.

These "ships of Tarshish" ("merchant ships" in more modern Bible versions), are suggested by some authorities as denoting a large trading vessel rather than one assigned to a particular place. In favour of this suggestion is that in the prophecies against Tyre the destruction of the ships of Tarshish is clearly taken to denote the demise of the whole merchant fleet rather than only those that sail to one particular location.

The other Tarshish was accessed from the Mediterranean Sea, as is shown when Jonah embarked for that destination from the port of Joppa (Jonah 1.3). Many places have been suggested as the location of biblical Tarshish, but it is most likely that Tartessus in modern Spain is being referred to. The Phoenician port of Tyre had many of these Tarshish ships (Isaiah 23.1), and among their imports from Tarshish was *"silver, iron, tin and lead"* (Ezekiel 27.12) – metals that are still being mined in southern Spain to this day. Tartessus was one of the Phoenicians' many trading centres in the western Mediterranean. Seguineau and Odelain suggest that "Tarshish" is simply a name for a distant land requiring sturdy ships to be reached from Israel (*Dictionary of Proper Names and Places in the Bible*. Odelain, O., Seguineau, R. Published by Robert Hale, London, 1982).

Did the Phoenicians trade with Britain?

It has long been suggested that Tarsus refers to Britain, another tin mining country. But it is questionable whether the Phoenician merchants ever regularly traded for tin as far away as Cornwall in south-west Britain. With easy access to plentiful supplies of tin in southern Spain it would not make economic sense to undertake the long sea journey along the Atlantic coast in their small boats, crossing the treacherous seas of the Bay of Biscay before reaching the Cornish coast. But this is not to say that Cornish tin did not come to the Mediterranean region. There is documentary and archaeological evidence of a flourishing Cornish tin trade with the Greeks, who greatly valued this commodity. The Greek historian, Herodotus, who lived in the 5th century BC called Britain *"Nesoi Kassiterides"* – "Tin Islands". But the Greek merchants avoided the dangerous Atlantic coast by shipping large ingots of tin across to France, then up the River Seine, by land across to the River Rhone and then by boat to the Mediterranean – thus avoiding the well-known dangers of the Bay of Biscay and any confrontation with the Phoenician traders near the Straits of Gibraltar.

The role of these nations

"Sheba, Dedan, the merchants of Tarshish, and all their young lions will say to you, 'Have you come to take plunder? Have you gathered your army to take booty, to carry away silver and gold, to take away livestock and goods, to take great plunder?'" (Ezekiel 38.13).

It is easy to take these nations' response as either threatening or engaging in active opposition to the invader. But once the design of the invader is apparent there is no mention of any active intervention. Admittedly it may be implied, but it is not stated.

Are Sheba, Dedan and the Tarshish merchants active opponents, merely onlookers, or even collaborators? We are left to ourselves to decide. Certainly there is no further mention of them, let alone of any results of their intervention.

Latter-day equivalents

As with all unfulfilled prophecies we must not be dogmatic as to any one outcome. We can only suggest what might happen in terms of the present situation whilst recognising that this could change very rapidly.

Sheba, Dedan and the merchants of Tarshish

The modern equivalents of these are undoubtedly the Gulf States, comprising of Bahrain, Kuwait, Oman, Qatar and the United Arab Emirates. These are extremely rich powers ruled by highly autocratic and seemingly anachronistic regimes. The policy of these nations has been to strengthen security ties with Western powers, in part by allowing the United States, France and the United Kingdom to build massive bases on their soil and by spending lavishly on Western arms.

Of recent years they have tended to stand aside from the various dissenting factions among their Arab neighbours in the Middle East, and their antagonism to Iran in particular has been quite pronounced. Although they have experienced some internal opposition stemming from the "Arab Spring", the power base of their rulers, for the moment at least, seems secure.

As we saw earlier, one of the two biblical places styled Tarshish is also in the same region, and the Gulf States amply fit the description of a merchant power.

If this is correct, then what of the KJV phrase *"all the young lions thereof"*? Young lions are often referred to in Scripture as powerful and energetic rulers (Jeremiah 2.15; Ezekiel 19.2–6). So maybe this is a reference to the powerful rulers of the Gulf States.

It is hard to argue a case for Tarshish to be modern Spain,

and as mentioned earlier the identification with the United Kingdom is very tenuous. Certainly, the association of the merchants of Tarshish with Sheba and Dedan, whose location is certain, suggests that all are from a similar part of the world.

Do the merchants of Tarshish actually withstand the northern invasion, or are they passive, even if vocal, onlookers? There may be depicted here the disapprobation of the northerner's invasion by the Gulf States but an unwillingness to intervene that is in keeping with their current policies. Or are we probing more than is justified in the light of our inherently defective understanding?

Chapter 7 The invasion of Israel

Whichever latter-day nations correspond to Sheba, Dedan and the merchants of Tarshish of Ezekiel 38 (as discussed in the previous chapter), it is clear that any intervention they make will be ineffectual. The northern invader's attack on Israel will initially be successful, as is repeatedly foretold: *"You will ascend, coming like a storm, covering the land like a cloud, you and all your troops and many peoples with you"* (Ezekiel 38.9); *"You will come up against my people Israel like a cloud, to cover the land. It will be in the latter days that I will bring you against my land"* (v.16). The success of the attack is also predicted by Zechariah: *"For I will gather all the nations to battle against Jerusalem; the city shall be taken, the houses rifled, and the women ravished"* (14.2). It would seem, therefore, that the invader gains complete control over Israel and Jerusalem.

How long will this occupation last, and what will characterise it? As with all unfulfilled prophecy, we cannot be sure, but Scripture gives us some points to consider.

It is easy to assume that the invader is destroyed immediately, and that within a short time Israel will enter its golden age under the rulership of Christ. But that would not humiliate the pride of Israel, which we believe is an essential part of the process. Prophecy sometimes gives an overall picture, with its component parts not necessarily following immediately after each other. An example of this is the single prophecy concerning Tyre (Ezekiel 26), part of which was fulfilled by the Babylonians, and the rest hundreds of years later by the Greeks.

Thus, it would seem from other prophecies that certain events will occur before Israel is extricated from the bondage of the invader. An awareness of this possibility might lessen our disappointment and the danger of our faith being undermined when these things actually happen.

A second captivity?

In connection with the latter-day attack there are a striking number of references to Israel going into captivity or, as in more recent translations, into "exile". The Zechariah reference already quoted continues: *"half of the city shall go into exile"* (14.2 RSV). Joel, when speaking of the time when God *"shall bring back the captives of Judah and Jerusalem"* (3.1), speaks of the invaders as having scattered Israel among the nations (v.2), sold their children (v.3), particularly to the Greeks, and having removed them far from their own border (v.6). The invaders will do to the Jews what they allegedly had done to the Palestinians – deprive them of their own land.

The reality of this yet future exile is confirmed when we note the many passages that refer to a return of exiles to Israel from the surrounding countries at the very time of the end. Such passages should not be confused with the well-known predictions of a general return from the centuries-long dispersion that has led to the formation of the present State of Israel.

For example, in Isaiah 11, after describing the blessings of Christ's future rule, when the "root of Jesse" will stand again on the earth, the prophet goes on to say: *"It shall come to pass in that day that the Lord shall set his hand again the second time to recover the remnant of his people who are left, from Assyria and Egypt, from Pathros and Cush, from Elam and Shinar, from Hamath and the islands of the sea. He will set up a banner for the nations, and will assemble the outcasts of Israel, and gather together the dispersed of Judah from the four corners of the earth"* (vv.11–12). So at the time of Christ's appearing there will be two regatherings: a "second time" from areas adjacent to Israel, followed by a gathering from the more distant "four corners of the earth". Are the more local returned exiles those that were displaced by the northern invader?

Similarly in Isaiah 27, in the day when God punishes the "Leviathan" (v.1), we read: *"And it shall come to pass in that day, that the Lord shall thresh from the channel of the r iver unto the Brook of Egypt, and you will be gathered one by one, O you children of Israel. So it shall be in that day, that the great trumpet will be blown; they will come who are ready to perish in the land of Assyria, and they who are outcasts in the land of Egypt, and shall worship the Lord in the holy mount at Jerusalem"* (vv.12–13). Here again is foretold a return from comparatively local countries at the time of the end. There is a similar reference in Zechariah 10.10–11.

So these prophecies of a yet future captivity into the surrounding nations, followed by references to a local return from exile at the return of Christ, confirm the possibility that the northern invader will indeed exile many of the Jews into Arab or Arab friendly areas. Have we therefore yet to witness some "ethnic cleansing", resulting in a forced migration of Jews out of Israel? Such mass movements of population are not unknown in recent times, as events in the Balkans demonstrated some years ago. If so, although the exile clearly will be only temporary, it will of necessity take some time. This suggests that the northern invader will be able to consolidate his position in Israel.

"Bring again the captivity"

As a little digression, we would mention that the KJV phrase "bring again the captivity of" does not always seem to have the meaning of a literal return from exile – although often this is included. For God also says that in the "latter days" He will "bring again the captivity" of Moab, Ammon and Elam (Jeremiah 48.47; 49.6,39 KJV). We are not aware of any Moabite captives awaiting return to Jordan. In more recent versions the original Hebrew word for "captivity" is usually translated as "fortunes" (RSV, NIV). Thus, the *Soncino Commentary* (1948) makes this observation: "The phrase 'turn the captivity' or 'bring about the captivity' is an idiom for 'restore the fortunes', a colloquial phrase for a general reversal of misfortune." It would seem, therefore, that confirmation from the context is desirable before we infer that "bring again the captivity of" necessarily refers to a physical migration back to a homeland.

Two thirds shall die

Although its application to the time of the end is not universally accepted, these words of Zechariah could be borne in mind as possibly relating to this time: *"And it shall come to pass in all the land, says the LOr D, that two-thirds in it shall be cut off and die, but one-third shall be left in it"* (13.8). The preceding verse seems to be a reference to the crucifixion of Jesus, yet the following one suggests that as a result of this punishment on Israel, the surviving third will come through the fire of God's wrath, be refined as precious metals and say: *"The LORD is my God"*. So a future application is not ruled out.

Israel's repentance necessary

It is a fairly well-established principle that God does not normally save people from a perilous situation until they cry to Him for help. Israel's history gives many examples of this. Jehoshaphat's plea in the face of the combined attack by Moab and Edom is a notable instance (2 Chronicles 20: this case is maybe even a foretaste of the actual future event we are considering) and others can be readily thought of. This principle is clearly set down by Joel. When a northern army attacks with devastating effect (Joel 2.1–11) then the prophet's advice to God's people is: *"'Now, therefore', says the LORD, 'Turn to me with all your heart, with fasting, with weeping, and with mourning.' So rend your heart, and not your garments; return to the LORD your God, for he is gracious and merciful, slow to anger, and of great kindness; and he relents from doing harm. Who knows if he will turn and relent… Blow the trumpet in Zion, consecrate a fast, call a sacred assembly; gather the people, sanctify the congregation, assemble the elders… Let them say, 'spare your people, O LORD, and do not give your heritage to reproach, that the nations should rule over them. Why should they say among the peoples, "Where is their God"'"* (vv.12–17).

If the northern invader proves to be Islamic, we can imagine the situation in Israel and Jerusalem after it has been overrun and punished because of their departure from God.

We can imagine many Jews dead or deported; their government superseded by a fanatical Islamic regime; the economy in ruins; retribution by the Palestinians for all the perceived wrongs of the previous Israeli administration a daily occurrence, so that the ordinary people fear for their very lives. The army is paralysed and the much-vaunted reputation of the Jews to defend themselves is in tatters. All its one-time allies and friends are, for some reason, powerless to help. And, after an initial optimism that things will soon change, the invasion seems to be getting permanent, and the nation of Israel destined for oblivion.

Is it in such extremity that Israel will realise that their only help is from the God who openly aided them in the past? Surely, almost in despair, they will then re-read the words of Joel inviting them to repent and to pray. Then they will be able to take comfort from God's assurance of a reply: *"Then the LOr D will be zealous for his land, and pity his people. The LOr D will answer and say to his people, 'Behold, I will send you grain, and new wine, and oil, and you shall be satisfied by them; and I will no longer make you a reproach among the nations: but I will remove far from you the northern army, and will drive him away into a barren and desolate land'"* (vv.18–20).

The prophecy of the seventy weeks

It may not seem at first sight that this prophecy has much relevance to the time of the end, predicting as it does the first coming of the Saviour. But as some suggest that it is an example of a prophecy with a built-in "gap" that stretches it out to include the time of the end it is worth considering here.

The context of the prophecy is that Daniel had prayed for the deliverance of Jerusalem: *"O Lord, according to all your righteousness, I pray, let your anger and your fury be turned away from your city Jerusalem, your holy mountain; because for our sins, and for the iniquities of our fathers, Jerusalem and your people have become a reproach to all that are around us"* (Daniel 9.16). In passing, we note that this description of Jerusalem's plight is equally appropriate to the future invasion.

In response to this prayer, Daniel was told that a period of seventy "weeks", or "sevens", was decreed concerning the Jews and the holy city: *"Seventy weeks are determined for your people and for your holy city, to finish the transgression, to make an end of sins, to make reconciliation for iniquity, to bring in everlasting righteousness, to seal up the vision and prophecy, and to anoint the Most Holy"* (v.24). This was a far-reaching prophecy that had its initial fulfilment in the work of the Messiah at his first coming, but clearly all its promised aspects could not be completely fulfilled until he returned.

Daniel was told that after sixty-nine weeks (or "sevens") the Messiah would come, after which he would be "cut off", and then the city would be destroyed (v.26). On a "day for a year" principle, here is a period of 483 years, after which the Christ would be revealed. This came to pass as recorded in the Gospels. The remaining week of the seventy was divided into two periods of three and a half days (years), with Jesus being sacrificed at the end of its first half (v.27). Christ's death brought to an end the necessity for animal sacrifices (v.27).

But what of the remaining half week, or three and a half years? It has been suggested that preaching to the Gentiles began at the end of the week – three and a half years after Jesus' death. But the next three and a half years after the crucifixion witnessed no significant fulfilment of the remaining aspects of the prophecy. It is also clear that the termination of the seventy weeks marks the end of the desolation of Jerusalem; the fate of Jerusalem being the main point of Daniel's prayer that was being answered by this prophecy.

It has therefore been suggested that the remaining half week, or three and a half days/years, which the angel said would terminate in the liberation of Jerusalem, relates to the time of the end. Such "gaps" are not uncommon in prophecy. For example, Isaiah 9.1–2 tells of the first coming of Jesus, but verses 3–7 jump forward to the establishment of the Kingdom, a gap of about 2000 years.

If this is correct, then can it be that the northerner's occupation of Jerusalem in the future that precedes its final liberation will last for the three and a half years? In this connection it is interesting that the same period of time is given in Revelation for a Gentile domination of the symbolic holy city: *"It is given unto the Gentiles: and they will tread the holy city underfoot for forty-two months"* (11.2). The next verse gives a similar period, this time describing it as 1260 days, for the period of the witnesses clothed in sackcloth. We (who are firmly wedded to the "continuous historical" view of the Apocalypse as the primary interpretation, whilst not excluding other secondary ones) are not suggesting that Revelation is here describing the future northern invasion or its duration; but even so the parallels are interesting and maybe significant.

"Time, two times and a half"

Using different terminology this same period of three and a half years occurs in Daniel 12.6–7: *"And I said to the man clothed in linen, who was above the waters of the stream, 'How long shall it be till the end of these wonders?' The man clothed in linen, who was above the waters of the stream, raised his right hand and his left hand toward heaven; and I heard him swear by him who lives for ever that it would be for a time, two times, and half a time; and that when the shattering of the power of the holy people comes to an end all these things would be accomplished."* This time-period has always been regarded as obscure in relation to the end-time prophesies, but could it be referring to the length of time that Daniel's people of the latter days would suffer the ravages of Gog's invasion? Then after a three-and-a-half-year period (a "time" being a year) the shattering of the power of the holy people would indeed come to an end, with the destruction of the invader.

So, to sum up, the northern invader will probably dominate Israel for some considerable time, possibly for over three years; but then, after Israel's true repentance, they will be delivered by divine intervention. This is the topic of our next chapter.

Chapter 8 The invader defeated

Israel's deliverance from the northern invader (or invaders) is one of the grand themes of the last-day prophecies, but just how it is to be achieved in practice is not easy to determine. In common with all prophecies relating to this time, the end is certain, but the steps by which it is reached are often indeterminate. There are many facets to the overall picture, and it is not easy to suggest how they all interact. For this reason, as always in this book, views are advanced which are of necessity tentative.

Our studies so far

In view of the somewhat extended nature of this study so far, it might be as well to summarise the points made in previous chapters. We first noted that we live in a world vastly different from that of our forebears, and the political map has had to be re-drawn. The fall of Communism and the greater integration of Russia into world politics and commerce, the development of European unity, the amazing recent rise in the influence of Islam and the worldwide threat of terrorism are developments that could not have been envisaged even a generation ago. The one unchanging element in this scene is the presence of Israel in the Middle East, but even now their security is being stretched to its limits in facing the Palestinian problem.

We then looked at prophecies describing latter-day attacks on Israel, and posed the question whether there was to be one attack or more. It was suggested that the Old Testament predictions more generally related to antagonism to the State of Israel, whilst the ones in Revelation refer to events after the establishment of Christ's rule and will consist of an attempt to overthrow him, this being the real Armageddon.

Later we tried to identify the invaders described in Ezekiel 38, and suggested that they represent the nations currently surrounding Israel, including the territories of states to the south of Russia, the majority of these being adherents of Islam. The success of the invasion was then examined, with the possibility of an ethnic cleansing of the Jews by their successful antagonists, leading to a temporary exile of some. It was also suggested that the invader's occupation of the land could last a considerable time. It is the outcome of the invasions that we look at in this chapter.

The prophets describe at least four ways by which the invader is overthrown, all of them an exhibition of the intense zeal and anger of Israel's God. But those who do not want to believe will be able to attribute at least three of these to natural causes:

1. Natural disasters.
2. In-fighting between the invaders.
3. Israeli aggression.
4. Direct divine intervention.

1. Natural disasters

Under this heading are several means by which the Gogian army will be destroyed.

First, there will be an earthquake: *"A great earthquake in the land of Israel… The mountains shall be thrown down, the steep places shall fall, and every wall shall fall to the ground"*

(Ezekiel 38.19–20); *"The heavens and the earth will shake"* (Joel 3.16); and the Mount of Olives will be split (Zechariah 14.4–5).

Second, the natural elements will be unleashed: *"I will rain down on him, and on his troops, and on the many peoples who are with him, flooding rain, great hailstones, fire, and brimstone"* (Ezekiel 38.22).

Third, by disease. Through Ezekiel God says: *"I will bring him to judgment with pestilence and bloodshed"* (v.22); and Zechariah speaks of: *"the plague with which the LOr D will strike all the people that have fought against Jerusalem"* (14.12).

2. In-fighting

Chronicles records that in Jehoshaphat's days God defeated the invading Ammonites and Moabites by in-fighting among the invaders, whilst Israel's armies looked on: *"The LOr D set ambushes against the people of Ammon, Moab, and Mount Seir, who had come against Judah; and they were defeated. For the people of Ammon and Moab stood up against the inhabitants of Mount Seir, to utterly kill and destroy them. And when they had made an end of the inhabitants of Seir, they helped to destroy one another. So when Judah… looked toward the multitude, there were the dead bodies fallen on the earth. Not one had escaped"* (2 Chronicles 20.22–24). In passing, we note that the "valley of Jehoshaphat" is also the scene of the latter-day invaders' defeat (Joel 3.2).

The future attackers will also suffer a similar experience,

for God will intervene *"as he fights in the day of battle"* (Zechariah 14.3). Ezekiel predicts: *"And I will call for a sword against him throughout all my mountains, saith the Lord GOD: every man's sword shall be against his brother"* (38.21), and Zechariah foretells: *"A great panic from the LOr D will be among them. Everyone will seize the hand of his neighbour, And raise his hand against his neighbour's hand"* (14.13).

In recent military campaigns so-called "friendly fire" has caused much anguish among the troops involved, but when this is directly influenced by the unseen hand of the Almighty, its effect will be devastating.

3. Israeli aggression

The number of references to Israel rising up to defeat the invaders is very impressive. Way back in the time of Moses, Balaam, in speaking of *"what this people* [Israel] *will do to your people* [Moab] *in the latter days"*, said: *"And Edom shall be a possession; Seir also, his enemies, shall be a possession, while Israel does valiantly"* (Numbers 24.14,18). This defeat by Israel of the latter-day Edom and Moab is confirmed by Isaiah in chapter 11. Speaking of the time when God will *"gather together the dispersed of Judah from the four corners of the earth"* (v.12) he goes on to say that: *"the adversaries of Judah shall be cut off; Ephraim shall not envy Judah, and Judah shall not harass Ephraim. But they shall fly down upon the shoulder of the Philistines toward the west; together they shall plunder the people of the East; they shall lay their hand on Edom and Moab; and the people of Ammon shall obey them"* (vv.13–14).

Jeremiah, in words that have never yet been fulfilled, has a similar prophecy. Speaking of Israel, God says: *"You are my battle-axe and weapons of war: for with you I will break the nation in pieces; with you I will destroy kingdoms; with you I will break in pieces the horse and its rider; with you I will break in pieces the chariot and its rider"* (51.20–21). Micah also predicts: *"And the remnant of Jacob shall be among the Gentiles, in the midst of many peoples, like a lion among the beasts of the forest, like a young lion among flocks of sheep, who, if he passes through, both treads down and tears in pieces, and none can deliver. Your hand shall be lifted against your adversaries, and all your enemies shall be cut off"* (5.8–9). In an earlier chapter of the same prophecy which, from the references to threshing, has a clear latter-day application we read: *"Now also many nations have gathered against you, who say, 'Let her be defiled, and let our eye look upon Zion'. But they do not know the thoughts of the LORD, nor do they understand his counsel; for he will gather them like sheaves to the threshing floor. 'Arise and thresh, O daughter of Zion; for I will make your horn iron, and I will make your hooves bronze; you shall beat in pieces many peoples'"* (4.11–13).

The prophecy of Zechariah has several references to Israel's combative role in the future. In the day that Jerusalem becomes a cup of trembling for the nations (12.2), God will: *"make the governors of Judah like a firepan in the woodpile, and like a fiery torch in the sheaves; they shall devour all the surrounding peoples on the right hand and on the left, but Jerusalem shall be inhabited again in her own place"* (v.6). And in the context of the future invasion we read in chapter 14: *"And Judah also will fight at Jerusalem"* (v.14).

This uniform testimony suggests that after an initial setback, the Israeli forces will be energised by God to complete the task begun by His deployment of the elements and by the in-fighting of the Jews' enemies.

No divine manifestation as yet?

We believe it is possible that, from the standpoint of the rest of the world, the reverses suffered by the invaders that we have considered so far, could be seen to be unfortunate coincidences rather than evidence of supernatural intervention. Storms, earthquakes and even volcanic eruptions of sulphur (brimstone) are not unknown in the area, and disease epidemics would naturally follow. Suspicions as to the dramatic success of the Israeli forces could well be raised, but it could be reasoned that since becoming a state they have a history of being successful against all odds.

We mention this because it is difficult to see (humanly speaking) how the nations would have the stomach to later reject and even fight against Christ if there was undeniable evidence of his presence and supreme power during the initial stages of the war against human rule. Crucial to this is the timing of the appearance of Christ to Israel and the world, as we consider next.

Chapter 9 Christ returns to Israel

In the previous chapter we suggested that four agencies will combine to bring about the destruction of the invaders of Israel:

1. Natural disasters.
2. In-fighting between the invaders.
3. Israeli aggression.
4. Direct divine intervention.

The first three were covered in chapter 8, leaving this chapter to concentrate on the fourth: direct divine intervention, as distinct from the outworking of providence implicit in the preceding agencies.

As with our earlier studies, there are many prophecies that relate to this time and it is not easy to see how they all interact. Thus, any suggestions as to a detailed sequence of events are offered conscious of our deficiencies in knowledge and understanding. But the involvement of the returned Jesus is not in doubt.

Separate advents to the saints and Israel

What seems clear, however, is that Christ will return separately to natural and to spiritual Israel. As far as his return to the saints is concerned, many have taken Paul's reference in 1 Thessalonians 4 to indicate that Christ's very first work at his return will be to raise the dead and gather them and the living to the judgement seat. This is taken as a fixed point in the timetable, and thus all other prophecies relating to the time of the end must refer to events after the resurrection.

This may well be the case, but we suggest that Paul's words cannot be used as definite proof of this. He said: *"For this we say to you by the word of the Lord, that we who are alive and remain until the coming of the Lord will by no means precede those who are asleep. For the Lord himself will descend from heaven with a shout, with the voice of an archangel, and with the trumpet of God. And the dead in Christ will rise first. Then we who are alive and remain shall be caught up together with them in the clouds to meet the Lord in the air. And thus we shall always be with the Lord"* (1 Thessalonians 4.15–17). Careful reading of his words shows that Paul is not here establishing that Christ's very first work at his return will be to raise the sleeping saints, but that *whenever the resurrection does occur*, the dead will rise before the living are called away, and then both will be gathered to Christ.

For the present study we will assume that by the time of Christ's manifestation to Israel the resurrection and judgement will be past, and that he will be accompanied by the redeemed in the events we now consider.

Christ's allusions to his return to Israel

Most of Jesus' own references to his return relate to his coming to his saints, but a few have a more general application. When he left Jerusalem and ascended from the mount of Olives (as the glory of God had done in Ezekiel's day: Ezekiel 11.23), a cloud received him, and the angels told the disciples: *"This same Jesus, who was taken up from you into heaven, will so come in like manner as you saw him go into heaven"* (Acts 1.11). Clouds feature constantly in predictions of Christ's second coming. Addressing his judges at his trial, Jesus said: *"I say to you, hereafter you will see the Son of Man sitting at the right hand of the power, and coming on the clouds of heaven"* (Matthew 26.64).

In response to their request for information on the "sign of your coming" Jesus said that: *"the sign of the Son of Man will appear in heaven, and then all the tribes of the earth will mourn, and they will see the Son of Man coming on the clouds of heaven with power and great glory"* (Matthew 24.30). Our Lord repeats this to John in Patmos: *"Behold, he is coming with clouds, and every eye will see him, even they who pierced him. And all the tribes of the earth will mourn because of him"* (Revelation 1.7). As far as Israel is concerned, this mourning will result in their acceptance of him as their Messiah: *"O Jerusalem, Jerusalem... Your house is left to you desolate; for I say to you, you shall see me no more till you say, 'Blessed is he who comes in the name of the LOrd!"* (Matthew 23.37–39).

It seems clear that Jesus will return in a way that will be visible to at least the nation of Israel, and will probably be associated with some heavenly manifestation and clouds.

Old Testament allusions to Christ's return

A direct reference to the place, mode and result of Christ's return is found in Zechariah. In confirmation of the angels' words to the disciples at his ascension we read: *"And in that day his feet will stand on the Mount of Olives, which faces Jerusalem on the east. And the Mount of Olives shall be split in two, from east to west, making a very large valley; half of the mountain shall move toward the north and half of it toward the south"* (Zechariah 14.4). The geographical changes to the area merit a separate study[1], but for this

---

[1] See *The Temple of the Future Age*, Peter J. Southgate.

consideration we note that Jesus returns to the same place from where he departed.

Israel's mourning

At some point during the northern armies' attack, the humbled Israelis will turn back to God. Possibly in their extremity they will recognise that their only hope lies with the God of their fathers. We again refer to the words of Joel; when speaking of a previous northern invasion (but which has clear application to the future one) he says: *"Now therefore, says the LOr D, turn to me with all your heart, with fasting, with weeping, and with mourning. So rend your heart, and not your garments; return to the LOr D your God… Gather the people, sanctify the congregation, assemble the elders, gather the children… Let the priests who minister to the LOr D, weep between the porch and the altar; let them say, Spare your people, O LOr D, and give not your heritage to reproach, that the nations should rule over them. Why should they say among the peoples, Where is their God?"* (2.12–17). Through Hosea, God also says repentance is essential to His return to Israel: *"I will return again to my place, till they acknowledge their offence. Then they will seek my face; in their affliction they will diligently seek me"* (5.15). Joel then describes the result of this penitence: *"Then the LOr D will be zealous for his land, and pity his people"* (2.18).

This mourning will be intensified when their heavenly visitor is identified as the one they crucified two millennia before. Dare we with reverence picture the scene? The awesome descent to Olivet of this august being, *"with power and great glory"*, will certainly attract the attention of the inhabitants of

Jerusalem, on whom by now God will have poured *"the spirit of grace and supplication"*. Will the *"house of David"* (the rulers) and the *"inhabitants of Jerusalem"* send out a deputation to enquire the identity of the visitor? They will then: *"look upon me [the one, NIV] whom they have pierced, and they will mourn for him, as one mourns for his only son, and grieve for him, as one that grieves for a firstborn"* (Zechariah 12.10).

This mourning will extend throughout the whole land (vv.11–14), and God's mercy will be shown to His people in the provision of a cleansing fountain to wash away their sin. During this time it may be that the Lord Jesus will have withdrawn himself – as he often did during his 40-day appearances to his disciples.

But with the cleansing fountain having done its work, God's people are now ready to receive their King. And so the impressive ceremony of welcome will take place. Christ's first triumphal entry into Jerusalem in the days of his flesh was but a foretaste of the time when they will cry: *"Blessed is he who comes in the name of the Lord"* (Matthew 23.39). In making this prediction Jesus was quoting from Psalm 118, which describes the joy and satisfaction of that happy day when Israel's rightful King is ushered into Jerusalem: *"Open to me the gates of righteousness; I will go through them, and I will praise the Lord.... The stone which the builders rejected has become the chief cornerstone. This was the Lord's doing; it is marvellous in our eyes. This is the day the Lord has made; we will rejoice and be glad in it. Save now, I pray, O Lord; O Lord, I pray, send now prosperity. Blessed is he that comes in the name of the Lord"* (vv.19–26).

As the welcoming procession nears the city gates the long-foretold dialogue between those outside and inside the city will take place:

"Lift up your heads, O you gates; and be lifted up, you everlasting doors; and the King of glory shall come in.

Who is this King of glory?

The LOr D strong and mighty, the LOr D mighty in battle. Lift up your heads, O you gates; and lift them up, you everlasting doors; and the King of glory shall come in.

Who is this King of glory?

The LOr D of hosts, he is the King of glory" (Psalm 24.7–10). Thus will the King of kings be welcomed into his capital city.

The wilderness of the people

But there are other Jews besides those in Israel, and these, too, will need to be incorporated into this new Kingdom of Israel. These are either ones who have been displaced by the northern invasion (see chapter 7) or who are longer-term exiles from the Holy Land. But just as those in the land would have suffered a purging process by the northern invasion, so these will need to undergo similar purification prior to their entry into Israel. Ezekiel suggests that these exiled Jews will be gathered towards the land of Israel, and en route be judged by God; only the suitably chastened being allowed to enter the new Kingdom of Israel. This is after the type of the original exodus from Egypt: *"And I will bring you out from the peoples, and gather you out of the countries where you are scattered, with a mighty hand, and with an outstretched arm, and with fury poured out. And I will bring you into the wilderness of the peoples, and there will I plead with you face to face. Just as I pleaded my case with your fathers in the wilderness of the land of Egypt, so will I plead my case with you, says the Lord GOD. And I will make you to pass under the rod, and I will bring you into the bond of the covenant; I will purge out from among you the rebels, and those who transgress against me: I will bring them out of the country where they sojourn, but they shall not enter into the land of Israel. Then you will know that I am the LORD"* (Ezekiel 20.34–38).

Where this "wilderness of the people" is situated, or whether it is a literal or figurative wilderness, is difficult to determine. But the final result of the judgements and purging will be that those allowed to remain in, or to enter, the land will become the first nation on earth cleansed in the sight of God, and consequently receive the fullness of His care and blessings.

The Lord shall roar out of Zion

Whilst all this is taking place in Jerusalem, it may be that the invading northern armies will still be licking their wounds in the more distant parts of Israel. Though reeling from the apparently fortuitous combination of natural disasters, friendly fire and a resurgent Israeli army (see chapter 8), they have still not given up hope of final victory.

But with the now invincible presence of Jesus in Jerusalem, their fate is sealed. Many prophecies describe the direct intervention of the Almighty, in the person of Christ, to eradicate the invader. This, we suggest, will be the first definite indication to the outside world of overt divine intervention in human affairs, even though at first they may not see it in this way. Here are just two references of many that could be selected: *"Then the LORD will go forth, and fight against those nations, as he fights in the day of battle"* (Zechariah 14.3); *"The LORD also will roar from Zion, and utter his voice from Jerusalem; and the heavens and the earth will shake: but the LORD will be a shelter for his people, and the strength of the children of Israel. So you shall know that I am the LORD your God, dwelling in Zion, my holy mountain. Then Jerusalem shall be holy, and no aliens shall pass through her again"* (Joel 3.16–17).

Thus, a preserved, chastened and purified Israel will become the head of the nations, and not the tail.

Chapter 10 Preaching the everlasting gospel: Revelation 14

In this study we come to the time when Christ has been acknowledged by Israel as their Saviour, and the northern invader of Israel has been finally destroyed when *"the LorD shall roar out of Zion"*. Jesus will then be installed as king in Jerusalem, accompanied by the redeemed saints. Prophecy suggests that then there will be a series of confrontations between this new ruler in Jerusalem and the rest of the world, resulting in the annihilation of all opposition to Christ and the establishment of him as supreme ruler on earth.

The sequence in Revelation 14

These confrontations between Christ and the remaining nations are symbolically depicted in Revelation 14, which, on the assumption that its events are to be taken sequentially, describes the various phases of Christ's subjugation of the rest of the world.

It opens with the picture of Christ and his redeemed singing a song of victory on Mount Zion (vv.1–5). Seven different activities then follow, involving six symbolic angels centred on the appearing of the Son of Man. The sequence is as follows:

Angel 1. Preaching the everlasting gospel (vv.6–7).

Angel 2. The fall of Babylon (v.8).

Angel 3. Warning not to worship the beast (vv.9–13).

Son of man on a cloud, with crown and sickle (v.14).

Angel 4. Harvest of the earth reaped (vv.15–16).

Angel 5. From temple, also with sickle (v.17).

Angel 6. Vintage of earth reaped (vv.18–20).

It will be readily seen that here is a clearly defined programme: these events following a definite pattern. An opportunity to repent will be followed by judgements on those who refuse. It also suggests that the transfer of power from human to divine rule will not be achieved rapidly, for God is never in a hurry.

These, then, are the various steps by which power on earth will be transferred from human to divine rule; and they contain a hint as to when Christ will openly manifest himself to the world at large, as distinct from Israel. A scriptural examination of this sequence will occupy the remainder of this book. The exposition will follow the general outline as proposed by John Thomas in *Eureka* vol. III, pages 398 onward (Birmingham 1912 edition), and readers may like to refer to these in following their own studies of the subject.

Preaching the everlasting gospel

The first event to follow the establishment of Christ as king in Jerusalem is depicted by an angel flying in *"the midst of heaven"* (v.6). This phrase is the translation of a single Greek word (*mesouranema*), which according to Liddell and Scott's *Lexicon* denotes "the meridian or zenith" – that is, the point at which the sun is highest in the sky. Another source describes it as meaning: "the highest point in the heavens, which the sun occupies at noon, where what is done can be seen and heard by all". Thus, the symbol seems to be saying that the angel has a universal message that all can hear, just as all can see the midday sun. In keeping with this, the rest of the verse states that the angel addresses *"every nation, tribe, tongue, and people"*.

The angel, or messenger, almost certainly represents the resurrected and redeemed saints. John was told that he *"must prophesy again about many peoples, nations, tongues, and kings"* (Revelation 10.11). The message, styled in the KJV "the everlasting gospel", does not seem to be primarily the message of the gospel of salvation through Christ as preached by the apostles. Rather, it is the good news that he has returned to establish the Kingdom, and to invite all nations to submit to him on pain of judgement. The definite article, "the", is not in the original, which describes the angel as "having *aionian* glad tidings to announce" (*Emphatic Diaglott*) or "having everlasting glad tidings" (Darby). As John Thomas clearly shows, the *aionian* glad tidings is news of the new ruler in Jerusalem who is about to establish the *aion*, or age, of the Kingdom.

The good news rejected

We can imagine these emissaries going forth from Jerusalem to every nation and religious system, inviting their submission to this new ruler in Jerusalem. In many ways this will be analogous to Moses appearing before Pharaoh demanding the release of God's people. The reaction then was: *"Who is the LORD, that I should obey his voice?"* (Exodus 5.2), and it will no doubt be similar in the majority of instances in the future. In Egypt, after Pharaoh's initial refusal, God hardened his heart so that the Almighty could bring upon him and his nation the intended punishment. All the signs and miracles that would have convinced an ordinary person were dismissed by that obsessed potentate.

And it will no doubt be the same when submission is demanded of modern nations. The world is ripe for severe judgements, and we can be sure that the rulers of the nations will be induced to defy Christ, even at the expense of reason, in order for them to receive the punishment that they deserve.

An impostor expected

From their perspective, human rulers, both political and religious, will see this person claiming to be king in Jerusalem as an impostor who will need to be defied and destroyed rather than obeyed. In this connection it is significant that the main Christian churches today, irrespective of their orientation, are expecting an antichrist to arise.

We remember over twenty years ago listening to a radio programme on the second coming of Christ. Various church leaders were interviewed, the majority accepting that Christ would return one day, but that it was so far in the future as to be irrelevant to life today. And one of the contributors, a bishop, said that Scripture taught that the return of Jesus would be preceded by an Antichrist appearing in Jerusalem, falsely claiming to be Jesus. This he based on 2 Thessalonians 2. He went on to say that it would then be the duty of the Church to resist and depose him. Only when this Antichrist was put out of the way, would the real Jesus return.

A one-time Catholic lady wrote making the same point: "When I was young I was brought up as a Catholic and one day in 1968 we asked the teacher to tell us about the end of the world. She was unable to tell us when it would happen.

But she said that at the time of the end someone would appear on the scene in Jerusalem claiming to be Christ and asking people to follow him. She said he would be extremely convincing, but far from being Christ he would be the Antichrist, the devil himself, and in fact the devil in Christ's clothing. She said that any that followed him would go to hell, and that only those who would resist him would be saved."

Similar stories are also promulgated on Internet religious websites. The Roman Catholics there say of the Antichrist: "Although much obscurity and difference of opinion prevails on this subject, it is generally admitted... that before the Second Coming there will arise a powerful adversary of Christ, who will seduce the nations by his wonders, and persecute the Church."

The Eastern Orthodox Church is also expecting a future ruler in Jerusalem, who will attempt to defeat Christianity. Their site proclaims: "All the growing aversion towards God on the part of mankind close to the end of the world will become, so to speak, concentrated in this definite man of sin, who will lead the final desperate battle against Christianity. Of the characteristics and actions of this Antichrist, we read in St Paul's second epistle to the Thessalonians... Then, on the murky waters of a global cataclysm, a 'brilliant' leader will surface as the sole saviour of mankind. Backing him will be a formidable organisation with the goal of global domination... The Antichrist will not be content with mere political authority and outward transformations. Praised by all, he will become so conceited that he will regard himself as a superhuman endowed with divine power. He will proclaim a new world-view – a new religion and new morality in place of 'outmoded' and 'unsuccessful' Christian teaching."

Mistaken identity

Thus, the real Jesus will be regarded as an impostor, whose destruction will be the sacred duty of all good Christians. This will be the final outworking of the words of the Spirit through Paul: *"God shall send them strong delusion, that they should believe the lie"* (2 Thessalonians 2.11). This alleged deceiver will in fact be Jesus, who being truly "endowed with divine power" will, as they say, "persecute the Church" and "proclaim a new world-view – a new religion and new morality in place of outmoded and unsuccessful Christian teaching."

We can imagine the reaction at such places as the Vatican and the European Union when Christ's emissaries demand their submission to this new ruler in Jerusalem. The threat relayed by these divine ambassadors – that "the hour of his judgment is come" – will, in the majority of cases, fall on deaf ears, and Christ's demand for their allegiance to him will be rejected. Thus, Christ and the human rulers of the world will be on a collision course, with an inevitable result.

Old Testament teaching

Psalm 2 is the Old Testament equivalent of Revelation 14 and displays the opposition of the "kings of the earth" and the "rulers" to the one of whom God says: *"I have set my king upon my holy hill of Zion"* (v.6). The message of the angel in mid-heaven of Revelation 14 is described in verses 10–12 of this psalm: *"Now therefore, be wise, O kings; be instructed, you judges of the earth. Serve the LorD with fear, and rejoice with trembling. Kiss the Son, lest he be angry, and you perish in the way, when his wrath is kindled but a little."*

The second angel

These invitations to submit being refused, the promised penalties will be exacted on the nations. This is depicted by activities of the remaining symbolic players in this drama.

The second angel proclaims that: *"Babylon is fallen, is fallen, that great city, because she made all nations drink of the wine of the wrath of her fornication"* (Revelation 14.8). Many Bible students believe that the Catholic Church, centred in Rome, is depicted by this symbol of Babylon. In the Old Testament several prophets used the same words to predict that literal Babylon of old would experience a sudden fall, and the second angel of Revelation 14 repeats some of their actual words: *"Babylon is fallen, is fallen; and all the carved images of her gods he has broken to the ground"* (Isaiah 21.9); *"Babylon has suddenly fallen and been destroyed"* (Jeremiah 51.8); *"Thus shall Babylon sink, and shall not rise from the catastrophe that I will bring upon her"* (v.64). An identical fate will befall spiritual Babylon: *"And he cried mightily with a loud voice, saying, 'Babylon the great is fallen, is fallen, and is become a habitation of demons, a prison for every foul spirit, and a cage for every unclean and hated bird"* (Revelation 18.2).

Thus, it would seem that this divine punishment will be directed against the so-called "eternal city". It is appropriate that the first target mentioned will be the centuries-old seat of the apostate Catholic power that has wrought such havoc among the true servants of God. The suddenness and completeness of this overthrow is predicted elsewhere in

Revelation. The destruction will come in "one day" (18.8), indeed in "one hour" (vv.10,17,19), and will involve fire and smoke (vv.8,9).

A literal fall?

From the use of the words "fall" and "sink", coupled with the allusion in Jeremiah that likens Babylon's fall to a stone plunging into water (Jeremiah 51.63–4), it is possible that Rome will literally be submerged. Scientists have recently noticed that Rome sits near an underground chamber of molten magma (hot molten rock) which is distorting the surrounding land surface and causing considerable anxiety to geologists. Is this a divinely appointed time-bomb, which at the appropriate time will erupt, spewing fiery molten rock, under which "Babylon the Great" will be eternally submerged?

There is a scriptural precedent for such drastic physical intervention. The cities of the plain were destroyed in a similar way, and grievous though the sins of Sodom and Gomorrah were, they have been vastly exceeded by those of the symbolic woman who has in her hand: *"a golden cup full of abominations and the filthiness of her fornication"* (17.4).

The timing of this destruction of Babylon in this sequence of events presents some difficulty, for, as is clear from later references, the papacy will be at the forefront of the opposition to Christ. If its administrative centre and power is destroyed at this early stage it is difficult to envisage it fulfilling this later role. Maybe the answer lies in the fact, so often seen in Scripture, that when God pronounces a thing it is as good as done, even though the actual deed is yet future. This is certainly true of Isaiah's words: *"Babylon is fallen, is fallen"* (21.9), for the fall did not actually occur until about 150 years later.

The fact that the next angel warns against worshipping "the beast and his image" also suggests that Rome is still active at the third stage of this divine programme outlined in Revelation 14. But this is the topic for our next chapter.

Chapter 11 The beast and its image: Revelation 14.9

In the previous chapter we listed the symbolic angels' activities that will take place either side of the public appearance of the returned Jesus:

Angel 1. Preaching the everlasting gospel (vv.6–7).

Angel 2. The fall of Babylon (v.8).

Angel 3. Warning not to worship the beast (vv.9–13).

Son of man on a cloud, with crown and sickle (v.14).

Angel 4. Harvest of the earth reaped (vv.15–16).

Angel 5. From temple, also with sickle (v.17).

Angel 6. Vintage of earth reaped (vv.18–20).

Having looked at the pronouncements made by angels 1 and 2 in chapter 10, we now proceed to the message of angel 3: *"Then a third angel followed them, saying with a loud voice, 'If anyone worships the beast and his image, and receives his mark on his forehead or on his hand, he himself shall also drink of the wine of the wrath of God, which is poured out full strength into the cup of his indignation. He shall be tormented with fire and brimstone in the presence of the holy angels and in the presence of the Lamb'"* (Revelation 14.9–10). This warning is contrasted with the faith of the saints and the blessedness of those who had suffered martyrdom: presumably at the hands of this "beast" (vv.12–13). Thus, this pronouncement presupposes the presence on earth at the return of Jesus of a false system of worship that should be rejected on pain of punishment.

What system in the latter days is represented by the "beast and his image"? This is what we will consider now. In suggesting an identification of the "beast" we must make a lengthy digression, going back to earlier parts of John's vision, and back in time to the earlier days of the Roman Empire. Chapters 12–13 of Revelation introduce us to three beasts: the dragon, the beast of the sea and the beast of the earth, the first two having many features in common.

The important thing to remember is that, according to the "continuous historical" interpretation of Revelation, these three describe the various phases which the Roman Empire has gone through since the days of John[2].

The dragon

The dragon of Revelation 12 represents the political organi-sation of the Roman Empire: *"And another sign appeared in heaven: behold, a great, fiery red dragon having seven heads and ten horns, and seven diadems on his heads"* (v.3). The seven heads depict two things about that organisation:

1) The seven mountains (Gk. *oros* also translated "hill"; see Matthew 5.14; Luke 4.29) on which the city of Rome was built (Revelation 17.9). For over 2000 years Rome has traditionally been called "the city on seven hills".

2) The seven forms of government (represented by the seven diadems, or crowns) by which Rome had been ruled during its long history (Revelation 17.10). There had been five different types of government prior to John's day, but in his times, and for several centuries after, Rome had an emperor. This imperial form of rulership was therefore the

---

[2] See *r evelation Explained*, by Peter J. Southgate and Clifford J. Wharton, chapters 12, 13 and 17.

sixth head of the dragon. This finally gave way to another form – the seventh head, but in John's day it had "not yet come". The ten horns remind us of the ten toes of Nebuchadnezzar's image of Daniel 2, which are usually taken to represent the various independent nations into which the iron Roman Empire would disintegrate. But at this stage in John's vision this division had not yet taken place – the crowns were on the heads, not on the horns.

This dragon – the political power of Rome – was originally pagan, but its idol worship was ousted and with the accession of Constantine in AD 312 the Empire became nominally Christian. This transfer is symbolically described in Revelation chapter 12. On his becoming emperor, Constantine moved his capital eastwards from Rome to his new city of Constantinople, modern Istanbul. Thus the dragon, the political power of the Empire, became centred on its eastern half. In about the year 400 the Empire was officially divided into eastern and western parts, with the Emperor's representative in Italy being stationed in Ravenna, not Rome. This left a vacuum of power that the next beast filled.

The beast of the sea

In Revelation 13 John saw two further beasts, which depict the situation in Rome and the western half of the Empire following the transfer of civil power to Constantinople. The first of these came up *"out of the sea"* (v.1) suggesting that the power it represented was centred on the Mediterranean seaboard.

The beast of the sea clearly depicts Rome (for it also

has seven heads and ten horns), but at a later stage in its history. The crowns are now on the horns, suggesting that the component states of the Empire are now independent. Also, verse 3, during the tenure of this power the reigning "sixth head" was fatally wounded – that is, rulership of Rome by an emperor came to an end. This occurred in AD 476, when the Goths from the north, under their king, Odoacer, conquered Rome, bringing the imperial "head" to a close and establishing the Gothic kingdom of Rome – the seventh "head", which was to last the "short space" of 70 years (17.10).

Another innovation was that, unlike the dragon, this beast of the sea represented a *religious* power, for "names of blasphemy" were on its heads. Further, this new power in Rome was to develop with the sanction of the political rulership in Constantinople: *"The dragon gave him his power, his throne, and great authority"* (v.2). This took place in AD 607, when the Emperor Phocas made the Bishop of Rome head of all Christian churches.

The sponsorship from the Roman Emperor in Constantinople (this eastern half of the Roman Empire still survived for about another thousand years) enabled the Bishop of Rome to extend his power until he became a political force as well as a religious one. In effect he reigned as an emperor, and thus it could be said that in Rome the deadly wound inflicted on the sixth (imperial) head of the beast had been healed.

So the beast of the sea depicts the power and influence of the papacy, in political as well as religious matters, as it developed after the demise of the western half of the Roman Empire. Although the emperor of the eastern part of the Empire had his representative in Ravenna up to about the year 750, as one writer says: "In 731 Gregory II cast off allegiance to Constantinople and the reign of the viceroys ended. The Rome of the Caesars was now to become the Rome of the Popes" (H.V. Morton, *A traveller in r ome*, 1960, p.132). Or, as an encyclopaedia says: "In Rome the pope was the real master" (*Encyclopaedia Britannica*, 1911, Art. Exarchate of Ravenna). And Thomas Hobbes, the Elizabethan philosopher (1588–1679), commented: "The Papacy is no other than the Ghost of the deceased Roman Empire, sitting crowned upon the grave thereof."

The beast of the earth

In the years that followed, nominal Christianity spread northward into central Europe, and at the same time the anti-Christian Muslim powers were developing in North Africa. In 732 the Moors crossed into Spain, a stronghold of papal influence. This invasion was repelled by the French ruler Charles Martell, thus earning the gratitude of the pope. Martell's son, Pepin, was crowned Emperor of France and Germany in 751, and he was able to come directly to the aid of the pope when Rome was attacked by the Lombards from northern Italy. The gratitude of the pope was increased when Pepin's son, Charlemagne, crushed the Lombards in 774 and – most significantly – donated their lands to the pope. The pope now owned a considerable amount of territory – later known as the Papal States – and by virtue of this became a confirmed political ruler as well as a religious one.

Charlemagne now ruled the greater part of Western Europe,

and in the year 800 the pope invited him to Rome, where he crowned him as emperor over what was later to be called the Holy Roman Empire. This further development of the original Roman power was an empire comprising Italy, France and Germany, and jointly ruled by the pope and the emperor. With an emperor ruling again in Rome, the sixth head could now be said to be well and truly healed. As one historian says: "So the Empire of Rome, which had died at the hands of Odoacer in 476, rose again in 800 as the Holy Roman Empire" (H.G. Wells, *The Outline of History*).

This Holy Roman Empire was symbolised by the beast of the earth: *"Then I saw another beast coming up out of the earth, and he had two horns like a lamb and spoke like a dragon"* (13.11). The symbols are very appropriate: an ostensibly lamb-like, that is, religious demeanour masked great political dragon-like power. The two horns depict the joint rulership of the pope and the emperor.

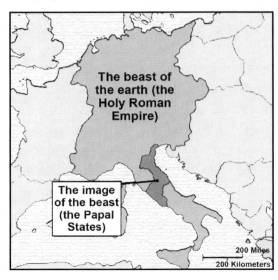

FIGURE 2
MAP SHOWING
THE EUROPEAN
SITUATION IN THE
MIDDLE AGES

With an emperor ruling again in Rome, the wounded sixth head of the beast of the sea could indeed be said to have been healed; but in another sense, as it came after the seventh or Gothic head, the Holy Roman Empire could also be described as the eighth head. This is of relevance to the time of the end, as we will see.

This Holy Roman Empire continued until 1806, when the European campaigns of Napoleon resulted in the abdication of the last emperor.

The image of the beast

One of the roles of the Holy Roman Empire was to boost the power and influence of the papacy, deceiving: *"those who dwell on the earth by those signs which he was granted to do in the sight of the beast, telling those who dwell on the earth to make an image to the beast who was wounded by the sword and lived"* (Revelation 13.14).

The word "image" does not refer to an idol, but rather denotes a "replica" – in this case of the beast of the sea. We recall that this beast was a blasphemous organisation that was ruled over by a system of rulership ("head") that had replaced a previously wounded one. This aptly describes the now autocratic rule of the pope in Rome, where he exercised all the power of the old emperors. And when Charlemagne gave him the Lombards' territory, forming the Papal States, the pope became a ruler in the conventional political sense.

Thus, this *replica* of the old order of things restored the old Roman system: now an all-powerful emperor ruled – but the emperor was the pope.

Forty-two months

The period over which the power of the papacy was to predominate is a symbolic 42 months (Revelation 13.5). Taking an average month as 30 days, and applying the day-for-a-year principle (cp. Numbers 14.34) this gives a period of 1260 years. Starting from the 607 decree that the Bishop of Rome was now head of the Church, we get to the year 1867. This was the time that the Italian patriot Garibaldi was uniting Italy. In 1870 the Catholic Church lost its Papal States, retaining only a small area on the Vatican hill at Rome, and the pope became the "prisoner in the Vatican". Thus, soon after the expiry of the 1260 years the pope ceased to be an overtly political ruler, although he has continued to exercise political influence by diplomatic means.

Summary

The beast of the sea, the beast of the earth and the image of the beast depict the political/religious organisation that developed and flourished in the countries bordering the Mediterranean and in Europe from the fall of the western Roman Empire in 476 until the nineteenth century, when its political power was taken away. We suggest that the three symbols do not represent separate organisations so much as the different phases of the Roman Catholic power during this period.

The beast and its image in the future

We can now return to the symbols of Revelation 14. The fact that the third angel warns those contemporary with the return of Christ not to worship the beast and its image implies that, despite its earlier reversal of fortunes, this symbolic beast will still be in existence and influential at the time of the end.

This is confirmed by the subsequent express statement that it is "the beast" that will initiate an attack on the returned Jesus: *"And I saw the beast, the kings of the earth, and their armies, gathered together to make war against him who sat on the horse and against his army"* (Revelation 19.19).

Also, in chapter 17 John describes the destruction of the great harlot, Babylon the Great, who rides on the beast that is: *"full of names of blasphemy, having seven heads and ten horns"* (v.3), that is, the beast of the sea. This beast will: *"make war with the Lamb, and the Lamb shall overcome them"* (v.14).

Other details are given of this symbolic beast. It is twice described as having an interrupted existence: *"The beast that you saw was, and is not, and will ascend out of the bottomless pit [Greek abyss] and go to perdition… they see the beast that was, and is not, and yet is"* (v.8). This is in accordance with the history we have examined. The Holy Roman Empire "was" until 1806, and the temporal power of the papacy also "was" until 1866 or thereabouts. At the moment both "are not", but prophecy suggests that they "shall ascend" and become powerful again.

We must therefore look for a revived power of the papacy that will, as considered in the previous chapter, oppose the claims of Jesus when he returns.

The eighth head

Where does Europe fit into this scenario? The prophecy of future events focuses on one particular phase of the past career of the beast. Earlier we noted that the Holy Roman Empire could be symbolically described in two ways. It represented the healed sixth head of the beast of the sea, that is, emperors ruled once more in Rome in the persons of the pope and Charlemagne and his successors. But chronologically the Holy Roman Empire followed the short-lived Gothic kingdom of Rome, represented by the seventh head. As it followed the seventh head, the Holy Roman Empire could also be said to be the eighth head. This reasoning is confirmed in chapter 17: *"The beast that was, and is not, is himself also the eighth, and is of the seven"* (v.11). Thus, future opposition to Christ will come from the revived "beast of the earth" phase of the symbols in Revelation 13.

Therefore, it seems that the Spirit is directing us to expect a revival of the old Holy Roman Empire – that relationship between the pope and Europe that was such a powerful influence centuries ago. And it is this combined power that will oppose Christ.

The current situation

Developments in Europe over the past 50 or so years are very relevant to these prophecies. We have witnessed the increasing integration of virtually all the European nations, with the possibility of a European super-state being openly canvassed. The collapse of the once-dominant Communist regimes has accentuated this process, and also allowed the previously suppressed influence of the Catholic Church to re-emerge.

It is fascinating to note that, in the eyes of the politicians involved, this process is a conscious attempt to resurrect the Holy Roman Empire as it was under Charlemagne.

Way back in 1950 Sir Winston Churchill said in the House of

Commons: "There can be no hope for a unified Europe without Germany, and there is no hope for Germany except within a free and united Europe ... in short, *the grand design of Charlemagne must be re-adapted to modern conditions.*" In 1955 the *Observer* wrote: "Western Europe is on the brink of federation. The plain truth is that the States are to pool their armies: France, W. Germany, Italy, the Low Countries will by that very act decide to scrap more than 1000 years of separate history, and become one State again, *as they were under Charlemagne*" (our italics in each case). This aim has been intensified in recent years. Under the proposed new European Constitution the EU: "will have become a sovereign state, in fact a federal superstate" (Ambrose Evans-Pritchard worldwatchdaily.org 7 July 2003).

The new emperor?

And all this is being done with the active support of the pope, who sees in the enlarged European Union a long awaited opportunity to revive his ancient influence. A warning note was sounded in an issue of the *Spectator* some years ago: "The issue of European religious union is one that has been concealed even deeper than the plans for political union, but the ratchet towards a Catholic Europe is just as real" (Adrian Hilton, "Render unto the Pope", 30 August 2003).

The pope's objective is that once the Protestant nations are committed to the emerging European superstate and its constitution, the Vatican plans to once again "Christianise" the European Union. As described by the *Sunday Telegraph*: "The Pope is calmly preparing to assume the mantle which he solemnly believes to be his divine right – that of new Holy Roman Emperor, reigning from the Urals to the Atlantic" (21 July 1991).

In 2004 the contribution of the pope to European unity was commemorated in a special award. Significantly, the city of Aachen, which was Charlemagne's capital, annually awards a Charlemagne Prize for one who its assessors decide has made the most significant contribution to European unity. That year it decided to award an Extraordinary Charlemagne Prize to Pope John Paul II. In their citation they say: "He draws our attention to the fact that the European Union can be an effective unity only if it promotes not only the economic and political values, but above all the spiritual and cultural values". Thus, the pope remains at the forefront of political and religious developments in Europe.

Many other commentators recognise what is happening and equate his rising power with the old Holy Roman Empire. In a major article entitled "Now, a Holy European Empire?" the *Sunday Telegraph* of 25 August 1991 wrote: "If European federalism triumphs, the EC will indeed be an empire. It will lack an emperor: but it will have the Pope."

There is much evidence that the European Union is rapidly becoming the resurrected Holy Roman Empire – the eighth head of the beast is ascending out of the abyss.

Thus, the stage is clearly being set for John's beast to "arise" and unite Europe in opposition to the one whom they deem to be an impostor, but who is in fact none other than the returned King of kings in Jerusalem. Meanwhile such a detailed fulfilment of prophecy strengthens our faith in the things that we have most surely believed.

In the next chapter we consider the fate of this unholy crusade.

Chapter 12 The vintage and the harvest: Revelation 14.14–20

In the previous chapter we listed the symbolic angels' activities that will take place either side of the public appearance of the returned Jesus:

Angel 1. Preaching the everlasting gospel (vv.6–7).

Angel 2. The fall of Babylon (v.8).

Angel 3. Warning not to worship the beast (vv.9–13).

Son of man on a cloud, with crown and sickle (v.14).

Angel 4. Harvest of the earth reaped (vv.15–16).

Angel 5. From temple, also with sickle (v.17).

Angel 6. From altar: earth's vintage reaped (vv.18–20).

So far we have looked at the pronouncements made by angels 1, 2 and 3. These symbols depict the invitation from the returned Jesus for all nations to submit to his rule, and the implied antagonism to Christ of the papal-led European nations – "the beast". At this juncture Jesus appears publicly on the world scene in a way that compels the nations to accept this new ruler in Jerusalem as the king of the whole earth: *"Then I looked, and behold, a white cloud, and on the cloud sat one like the Son of Man, having on his head a golden crown, and in his hand a sharp sickle"* (Revelation 14.14). The crown proclaims him as King of kings and the sickle implies that he is coming to judge the offenders.

Angels from the temple and altar

Angels 4–6 depict these judgements, the first two using the

symbol of a harvest, and the last that of a winepress. The first two are described as coming out of the temple in heaven, implying a direct commission from God to avenge human wickedness that has been an affront to His righteousness (cp. chapter 16.17).

Why does the final angel (14.18) come from the altar? We suggest that it is a reference back to the sixth seal, where Christ's true martyrs under the altar are depicted as pleading for vengeance: *"When he opened the fifth seal, I saw under the altar the souls of those who had been slain for the word of God and for the testimony which they held. And they cried with a loud voice, saying, 'How long, O Lord, holy and true, until you judge and avenge our blood on those who dwell on the earth?'"* (6.9–10). Those cries will be answered when the final judgements are poured out on the systems that down the ages have persecuted and killed the saints.

Harvest and vintage

Reaping, threshing and treading out grapes in a winepress are frequent scriptural figures for divine judgements. All these processes involved physical assault on the crops. Wheat was cut with a sickle, and the ears were trampled by animals or by using a threshing sledge to release the grain. The unwanted chaff was then blown away by the wind. Grapes were cut from the vine, placed in a rock-hewn pit and then heavily trampled on to release the juice.

These violent procedures are apt symbols of the punishment of nations, especially when, as here, *"the harvest is the end of the age; and the reapers are the angels"* (Matthew 13.39). Joel, speaking of the time of the end, combines the images of harvest and winepress when the Lord's "mighty ones" are given this invitation: *"Put in the sickle, for the harvest is ripe. Come, go down; for the winepress is full, the vats overflow – for their wickedness is great"* (3.13). Jeremiah, speaking of ancient Babylon, but with a clear reference to her modern counterpart, says: *"The daughter of Babylon is like a threshing floor, when it is time to thresh her… and the time of her harvest will come"* (51.33). Similar imagery is used in Isaiah of the returned Jesus: *"I have trodden the winepress alone; and from the peoples no one was with me. For I have trodden them in my anger, and trampled them in my fury. Their blood is sprinkled upon my garments, and I have stained all my robes"* (63.3); or by Habakkuk: *"You marched through the land in indignation; you trampled the nations in anger"* (3.12).

The result of these judgements is graphically described by Daniel. Speaking of the components of the great metallic image that represented kingdom of men, he says: *"Then the iron, the clay, the bronze, the silver, and the gold were crushed together, and became like chaff from the summer threshing floors; the wind carried them away so that no trace of them was found"* (2.35). Combining these passages we can see that the symbols in Revelation of treading grapes, reaping, threshing and blowing away the chaff have a firm basis in the Old Testament prophecies.

"Power over fire"

An additional ingredient of these judgements will be fire: the angel that came from the altar *"had power over fire"* (v.18), which will be another agent in the punishment of the world at Christ's return. Again, this symbol is firmly based on Old Testament predictions of the last days: *"Upon the wicked he will rain coals; fire and brimstone and a burning wind shall be the portion of their cup"* (Psalm 11.6); *"For behold, the LORD will come with fire and with his chariots, like a whirlwind, to render his anger with fury, and his rebuke with flames of fire. For by fire and by his sword the LORD will judge all flesh; and the slain of the LORD shall be many"* (Isaiah 66.15–16). And, in addition to the many references to punitive fire in Revelation, the New Testament describes the same method of purifying the earth: *"But the heavens and the earth which are now preserved by the same word, are reserved for fire until the day of judgment and perdition of ungodly men"* (2 Peter 3.7).

A warning for us

A consideration of these symbols should impress on the true followers of Christ the terrible severity of the judgements that will be inflicted on the earth after Jesus manifests himself to the world. As Isaiah predicted: *"Therefore the curse has devoured the earth, and those who dwell in it are desolate. Therefore the inhabitants of the earth are burned, and few men are left"* (24.6). It was no mere platitude when Jesus bade his followers: *"Watch therefore, and pray always that you may be counted worthy to escape all these things that will come to pass, and to stand before the Son of Man"* (Luke 21.36). The solemn inference is that those who are not ready for his return will not escape, but be made to share in the judgements of this fearful time.

What will actually happen?

Having discussed the symbols used to describe these events, we now consider how they may work out in practice.

As always when looking to the future, we do so conscious of our limited understanding and the recognition that events may turn out to be very different from what we envisage. However, the overall picture seems clear. There is good evidence that there will be rejection of the "everlasting gospel" preached by the first angel in chapter 14, followed by a united attack by human powers on Christ's administration in an attempt to unseat him from his newly established throne in Jerusalem. This attack is probably the trigger for the judgements inflicted by the remaining angels of Revelation 14.

Old Testament predictions

As already mentioned, Psalm 2 describes the insurrection against the king whom God has established in Jerusalem: *"Why do the nations rage, and the people plot a vain thing? The kings of the earth set themselves, and the rulers take counsel together, against the Lord and against his Anointed, saying, 'Let us break their bonds in pieces and cast away their cords from us'"* (vv.1–3). But this opposition will prove futile, and the Psalm continues by saying that this plotting will be followed by God's "deep displeasure" as symbolised by the judgements in Revelation 14: *"He who sits in the heavens shall laugh; the Lord shall hold them in derision. Then he shall speak to them in his wrath, and distress them in his deep displeasure"*. The result of this confrontation is beyond doubt: *"Yet I have set my King on my holy hill of Zion"* (Psalm 2.1–6).

We suggest that the latter half of Joel 3, with its reference to harvesting with sickles and pressing out grapes, also refers to this time. A holy war is proclaimed by the nations, and God responds by sending down His "mighty ones": *"Proclaim this among the nations: 'Prepare* [Heb. *qadash,* "sanctify"] *for war, wake up the mighty men, let all the men of war draw near, let them come up… Assemble and come, all you nations, and gather together all around: cause your mighty ones to come down there, O LORD'"* (Joel 3.9–11).

New Testament predictions

When we turn to a later chapter in Revelation we have God's "mighty ones" depicted in more detail. The brief reference in chapter 14 to the Son of Man on the cloud is expanded in chapter 19 into symbols of a fully equipped and invincible army. John saw: *"heaven opened, and behold a white horse; and he who sat upon him was called Faithful and True, and in righteousness he judges and makes war. His eyes were like a flame of fire, and on his head were many crowns. He had a name written, that no man knew, except himself. And he was clothed with a robe dipped in blood, and his name is called The Word of God. And the armies in heaven, clothed in fine linen, white and clean, followed him upon white horses. Now out of his mouth goes a sharp sword, that with it he should strike the nations. And he himself will rule them with a rod of iron. He himself treads the winepress of the fierceness and wrath of Almighty God. And he has on his robe and on his thigh a name written: KING OF KINGS, AND LORD OF LORDS"* (Revelation 19.11–16).

This vision of the awesome power of Jesus and his saints brings together many of the aspects of divine judgement that we have already considered – fire, a winepress, blood-spattered clothes and a sharp weapon. But who are his opponents? In words that echo the ideas and even the phraseology of Psalm 2, we are told that it is *"the beast and the kings of the earth"*: *"And I saw the beast, the kings of the earth, and their armies, gathered together to make war against him that sat on the horse, and against his army"* (Revelation 19.19).

Opposition by Church and State

In previous chapters we have identified the "beast" as the Holy Roman Empire in its resurrected form: that is, the united nations of Europe. Seated on this beast will be the woman that represents spiritual Babylon (Revelation 17). It is this confederacy of Church and State that will attempt to dethrone Christ and the saints. As Paul predicted: *"Then the lawless one will be revealed, whom the Lord shall consume with the breath of his mouth and destroy with the brightness of his coming"* (2 Thessalonians 2.8).

It is not difficult to imagine a possible scenario. Almost throughout its long history the Roman Catholic Church has been on its guard against the arrival of an Antichrist who would attempt to destroy it. Therefore that church has had a long tradition of organised opposition to any who may appear in this role. It has always been believed that the Antichrist would appear in the Holy Land, and so the First Crusade was initiated, to expel the Turks and Saracens. An additional factor in these medieval crusades was the occupation of the so-called "holy places" in Jerusalem and its vicinity by those they considered infidels.

When Christ appears, claiming to be the new king of Israel, it is easy to see that the papacy will view Jesus as the embodiment of the Antichrist, and so – on the basis of previous crusades – invite its adherents to a holy war to depose this supposed infidel and to free what they consider to be the holy places. The symbols of Revelation suggest that the majority of Europe will support this campaign.

It seems almost incredible that the religious leaders will be so blind that they will not be able to see their monumental error in their assessment of this new ruler in Jerusalem. But blindness in the face of evidence is the hallmark of men determined to retain their hold on power. It was so in the case of the Jewish leaders in Christ's original ministry. Undeniable miracles, even the resurrection of the decaying corpse of Lazarus, failed to penetrate their obsessive determination to demonstrate that they were right. And it will be the same in the future. As Paul said in this very connection: *"God will send them strong delusion, that they should believe the lie"* (2 Thessalonians 2.11).

Gathering to Armageddon

This opposition will take the form of a military campaign, but we can only conjecture the details. All we are told is that the combined religious and civil powers – the beast, and the kings of the earth and their armies – will gather to make war on Christ. But there are two hints that may suggest that the rebels will advance at least as far as northern Israel. The first may be contained in Revelation 14.20. Speaking of the judgements executed by the final angel, we read: *"And the winepress was trampled outside the city, and blood came out of the winepress, up to the horses' bridles, for one thousand and six hundred furlongs"*. It has been pointed out that 1600 furlongs is about the length of the land of Israel, and maybe the symbol indicates this as the "winepress".

Second, in Revelation 16.13–16 we read that, as a result of influences emanating from the "dragon", the "beast" and the "false prophet", the *"kings of the earth and of the whole world"* were *"gathered… together into a place called in the Hebrew tongue Armageddon"*. Here, as John Thomas shows in *Eureka* vol. III, the word "Armageddon" can be symbolic, translated as "a heap of sheaves in the valley for threshing" – thus continuing the idea of threshing as a punitive process. But as well as being a symbolic name, the reference to the Hebrew tongue may suggest that a location in Israel is indicated. If this is so, the place of this final conflict is possibly the Plain of Esdraelon in northern Israel.

This is the real Armageddon, *"the battle of that great day of God Almighty"* (Revelation 16.15), and in our view this term should never be applied to the Gogian invasion of Ezekiel 38.

The rebels destroyed

Wherever it takes place, the result of the conflict is certain: *"And the beast was captured, and with him the false prophet who worked signs in his presence, by which he deceived those who received the mark of the beast and those who worshipped his image. These two were cast alive into the lake of fire burning with brimstone. And the rest were killed with the sword which proceeded from the mouth of him that sat on the horse. And all the birds were filled with their flesh"* (Revelation 19.20–21).

The dragon survives

The religious elements of the old Roman Empire – symbol-ised by the beast, its image and the false prophet – are thus completely destroyed in the "lake of fire"; but the purely political organisation, the dragon (see page 79), will be permitted to continue into the Millennium, although under severe restraints (Revelation 20.1–3). This is in keeping with the situation described in Daniel 7. Here is described the dreadful and terrible fourth beast, which speaks *"pompous words against the Most High"*. The various features of this beast clearly identify it with the beast of Revelation 19. Daniel's fourth (Roman) beast was consigned to *"the burning flame"* (7.11). But at the time when *"one like the Son of Man"* came *"with the clouds of heaven"* (cp. Revelation 14.14) and the *"saints possess the kingdom"* we are told that Daniel's other beasts *"had their dominion taken away: yet their lives were prolonged for a season and time"* (Daniel 7.12,13,22). In his *Exposition of Daniel* John Thomas suggests that this is a code for 1000 years: "A season and a time, then, is 1000 years, or two times of 360 years each; and a *set time* of 280 years; or nine months and ten days of years; 280 days being a set time, or period of gestation" (p.21).

This prediction of taking away the dominion and prolonging the lives of Daniel's beasts for 1000 years has its counterpart in Revelation 20. The dragon, the political as distinct from the religious influence, is to survive though it is bound for the thousand years (Revelation 20.3). This dragon then being released from its prison suggests that the uprising at the end of the Millennium will therefore have political, not religious, objectives. The result will be the complete annihilation of any human attempts at rulership. The dragon will then share the same fate as befell the beast and false prophet a thousand years earlier (Revelation 20.7–10) and Christ will reign without any opposition.

This study provides great encouragement for true followers of Christ. Having been redeemed and purified by the blood of Jesus, they hope to be among those symbolic armies that follow Jesus upon white horses, clothed in fine linen, white and clean. As the Psalmist said: *"Let the saints be joyful in glory; let them sing aloud on their beds. Let the high praises of God be in their mouth, and a two-edged sword in their hand, to execute vengeance upon the nations, and punishments upon the peoples; to bind their kings with chains, and their nobles with fetters of iron; to execute on them the written judgment – this honour have all his saints. Praise the Lor D"* (Psalm 149.5–9).

Chapter 13 The kings of the north and south

So far we have not referred to the prophecy in Daniel chapters 10–12, which foretells events that have long been regarded as describing stages leading up to the return of Christ and the setting up of the Kingdom. For completeness we shall consider it now.

After a three-week period of mourning and fasting Daniel had a vision of a glorious being who revealed to him the future of the Jewish people: *"Now I have come to make you understand what will happen to your people in the latter days, for the vision refers to many days yet to come"* (Daniel 10.14). His message depicted the events from Daniel's day right up to the return of Christ and the setting up of the Kingdom. It is important that they are read as one prophecy. *Speakers' Commentary* observes: "The division into chapters 10, 11 and 12 is unfortunate and inconvenient. The whole section forms one connected whole, and to be understood must be read regardless of the current divisions."

The focus on Jewish events in these chapters is in keeping with the main divisions of the prophecy of Daniel. The first seven chapters are mainly written in Aramaic, and are concerned primarily with the politics and events of the Gentile nations. The rest of the book is written in Hebrew and concentrates on the fortunes of the Jewish nation. This should always be borne in mind when attempting to decipher the relevance of the message.

The other thing to bear in mind is that the events foretold in this very extensive prophecy – covering over 2500 years –

cannot be completely continuous. There must be some gaps where large portions of history have to be jumped over. This is not an uncommon feature of far-reaching predictions – for example in the Olivet prophecy and in many cases in Isaiah (see page 77).

But remembering that this section of Daniel is all one prophecy and the chapter divisions and indeed the para-graph marks are not in the original, having been added in line with the opinions of the translators or later editors, it is sometimes difficult to determine where these gaps occur.

The angel commenced the prophecy by saying that: *"three more kings will arise in Persia* [they were Ahasuerus, Artaxerxes and Darius], *and the fourth* [Xerxes] *shall be far richer than them all"* (11.2). This fourth king, Xerxes, was to "stir up" his army against the rising Greek power, but Persia would later be defeated by the "mighty king" Alexander the Great, and the Greek Empire would replace the Persian one (vv.2–3). This occurred in 330 BC. On Alexander's death it was said that: *"his kingdom shall be broken up and divided toward the four winds of heaven"* (v.4). This happened because Alexander had no son and his empire was divided among his four generals. Soon, those controlling the northern section (the Selucid rulers in Syria) and the southern kingdom (the Ptolomies in Egypt) would absorb the others, making two dominant opposing powers, the king of the north and the king of the south.

History from 330 to 164 BC

The rest of chapter 11, up to verse 35, predicts in great detail the various activities of these two powers over the next two centuries. It is a wonderful example of divine foreknowledge, and as such should be a source of great comfort in the foreknowledge of God. For a résumé of the historical fulfilment of these verses, see John Thomas' *Exposition of Daniel*, Section 16.

With the events foretold in verses 34–35 we arrive at the time of the successful Maccabean revolt against the Selucid king of the north in 164 BC, when the Jews were *"aided with a little help".*

Up to this point in the chapter there is little divergence of opinion by expositors on how the prophecy has been fulfilled, but from then onward there is less agreement. Verses 36–39 are regarded by some as describing a power that will dominate in the earth for over 2000 years until the "time of the end" (v.40), when *"the wrath has been accomplished"* and *"what has been determined shall be done"* (11.36). Others, aware of the angel's purpose to inform Daniel of the history of the Jews, restrict the prophecy to the events leading up to the destruction of Jerusalem in AD 70.

The identity of the king

Any interpretation hinges on the identity of the one styled "the king" in the following reference: *"Then the king shall do according to his own will: he shall exalt and magnify himself above every god, shall speak blasphemies against the God of gods, and shall prosper till the wrath has been accomplished; for what has been determined shall be done. He shall regard neither the God of his fathers nor the desire of women, nor regard any god; for he shall exalt himself above them all. But in their place he shall honor a god of fortresses;*

and a god which his fathers did not know he shall honor with gold and silver, with precious stones and pleasant things. Thus he shall act against the strongest fortresses with a foreign god, which he shall acknowledge, and advance its glory; and he shall cause them to rule over many, and divide the land for gain" (11.36–39).

To understand this section of the prophecy it is important to identify this notable king that was to come on the scene. This ruler is not given the title of either king of the north or king of the south, and presumably is therefore a different ruler. There are several possible suggestions – all of which have some problems.

The similarity of language to that of 2 Thessalonians 2.7–9, which also speaks of a blasphemous and self-aggrandising ruler, has led many to suggest that here is a reference to the pope and the system that he heads: *"Let no one deceive you by any means; for that Day will not come unless the falling away comes first, and the man of sin is revealed, the son of perdition, who opposes and exalts himself above all that is called God or that is worshiped, so that he sits as God in the temple of God, showing himself that he is God"*.

This is the interpretation given by John Thomas, referring it to the progressive powers that dominated Judah from the Maccabean time forward until the establishment of the Kingdom. In this interpretation the pagan Roman Empire was initially "the king" after it defeated the Selucid kingdom, but it later assumed its blasphemous papal identity when the Holy Roman Empire was set up by Charlemagne in 800. This, he said, equates with the little horn of the goat of Daniel 8.9–12, which was to invade "the glorious land", to exalt *"himself as high as the Prince of the host"* and to take away the "daily sacrifices". This "little horn" is a clear reference to the Roman power that would arise out of the fourfold fragmentation of the Greek Empire. From this developed the Roman Catholic system that continues to the present day. This power becomes the king of the north of verse 40.

There is another possibility that can be considered: one that does not necessarily exclude the above. The fact that "the king" is introduced into the prophecy immediately after the times of the Maccabees has led others to feel that a more immediate fulfilment is preferable, especially as the Jewish nation, as such, did not exist during the later papal times. Certainly, in the other scriptural predictions of the last days no one termed "a king" is depicted as opposing the Jewish people. Thus, it has been suggested that Herod the Great is being described in verses 36–39, this powerful king fulfilling the various angelic descriptions of the king's reign and character. He certainly did *"according to his own will"* (the same is said of Alexander the Great in v.3); he *"magnified himself"*; and by his actions he *"blasphemed the God of gods"* (v.36). He honoured the God *"his* [Idumean] *fathers did not know"* with *"gold and silver, with precious stones and pleasant things"* (v.38) when he lavishly restored the temple at Jerusalem. History records that he built many "fortresses" to defend his realm. He accepted a "foreign god" (v.39) when he, like most of those in the Roman Empire, worshipped the emperor as divine.

Terms such as "the last days"

It would be helpful at this juncture to consider some similar scriptural terms denoting the termination of certain periods, as an aid to understanding what epoch of God's programme is indicated.

There are several ways used by Scripture to indicate the ends of particular phases of the divine programme. Terms such as "the time of the end", "the end", "the latter days" or "the last days" occur throughout the Old and New Testaments. Not all of these are speaking of the days immediately before the setting up of the Kingdom. The context of the term usually determines which "end" is being referred to.

For example, when Isaiah prophesies that: *"It shall come to pass in the latter days, that the mountain of the Lor d's house shall be established on the top of the mountains"* (2.2), and when Martha said of Lazarus: *"I know that he shall rise again in the resurrection at the last day"* (John 11:24), then events at the return of Christ are being described. Paul's words: *"then comes the end"* (1 Corinthians 15.24) speak of another event even beyond the Millennium.

Alternatively, when the disciples asked Jesus about the "end of the age" he gave them the Mount Olivet prophecy, where he answered their query, initially at least, by predicting the events surrounding the fall of Jerusalem in AD 70 (Matthew 24.3,6,14; Luke 21.9). Daniel also describes the fall of Jerusalem as being at "the end", when the *"people of the prince* [the Romans] *that shall come shall destroy the city and the sanctuary"* (9.26). A quick look at a concordance will show that the prophecy of Daniel has several other references to an "end", but not all refer to the events at the return of Christ. In the letter to the Hebrews, written in the middle sixties AD the phrase "these last days" clearly refers to the years just prior to AD 70 (1.2), and later says that Christ's death was *"at the end of the ages"* (9.26).

In confirmation of this John Thomas writes: "The things recorded in the eighth and ninth chapter gave Daniel more particularly to understand what should befall Judah and Jerusalem in 'the last days' of the Mosaic constitution of things" (*Exposition of Daniel* p.45).

The "time of the end" of Daniel 11.40

Which "time of the end" is referred to in Daniel 11.40? Here we come to the point we made earlier, that somewhere in the historical sequence depicted by the prophecy there must be a time gap. Most interpreters place this gap at the beginning of verse 40, which commences with the phrase *"At the time of the end"*.

As already mentioned, the angel's purpose in revealing the future was particularly to tell Daniel what would happen to his people – the Jews: *"to make you understand what is to befall your people in the latter days. For the vision is for days yet to come"* (10.14, RSV). Hence, the detailed predictions of the events in the time of the end of verse 40 could equally be either the end of the Jewish national existence in AD 70 – an event that has already been referred to in Daniel – or the events that immediately precede the establishment of the Kingdom. We will consider these two options next.

A yet future time of the end

Those who understand the events of verses 40–45 as describing the future attack by the king of the north being that of Gog and his allies (Ezekiel 38–39) believe that there is a gap of approximately 2200 years between verses 39 and 40. Thus, the attack of the king of the north is still awaited. The Gogian power will attack Israel: *"like a whirlwind, with chariots, horsemen, and with many ships; and he shall enter the countries, overwhelm them, and pass through. He shall also enter the Glorious Land, and many countries shall be overthrown; but these shall escape from his hand: Edom, Moab, and the prominent people of Ammon..."* (Daniel 11.40–41), but will come to an untimely end.

It is believed that this northern power will occupy ancient Constantinople (modern Istanbul) and thus assume the territory and the role of the old Roman Empire, so becoming the king of the north. Like that previous empire in AD 70 this modern power will descend on Jerusalem with destructive fury, and establish its headquarters there. The invader will overflow into Egypt, looting its treasures, but Edom, Moab and Ammon, the trans-Jordan countries, will escape the onslaught. The invader will be destroyed, coming to his end with no one to help him.

Correctly ignoring the chapter division, this interpretation regards the standing up of Michael, the great prince, that is, Jesus, as occurring at his return to earth. He will then instigate an unprecedented time of trouble on the world, after which the resurrection, judgement and glorification of the faithful will take place.

There are very good grounds for this interpretation, but, whilst it seemed very probable in the middle of the nineteenth century, it does raise some difficulties in light of the situation in the twenty-first.

An attack by the king of the south

The northerner's attack is to be in response to an initial one by the king of the south: *"At the time of the end the king of the South shall attack him"* (v.40). Around 150 years ago this was confidently understood as referring to the British power – whose might and influence dominated the whole world at that time. The building of the Suez Canal – considered a lifeline for British commercial interests – meant that as the Turkish Empire "dried up" Britain considered it essential to have a presence in Egypt. In 1882 Britain occupied Egypt, and remained a dominant influence there for another 70 or more years. In this way, Britain was considered to be the king of the south, who was expected by some action to initiate the king of the north's invasion.

But that situation has not applied for many decades, and at the time of writing Egypt is an independent, poverty-stricken country racked with civil strife and with a weak government that would hardly commence an attack on a vastly superior power a few hundred miles to the north. Nor does it possess the *"treasures of gold, silver… and precious things"* (v.43) that would incite the cupidity of the northern invader. And as Egypt is now part of a large bloc of Arab nations, it is very unlikely that another power will impose itself on that country to assume the mantle of the king of the south. The possibility that things may rapidly and fundamentally change cannot, of course, be ruled out, but there is little sign of this as yet.

Ignoring for the moment the problem that today there seems to be no king of the south to prod the king of the north, this understanding of Daniel 11.40–45 envisages that here is the invasion of Israel as described in Ezekiel 38–39. And at this juncture (again remember there are no chapter divisions in the original): *"Michael shall stand up, the great prince who stands watch over the sons of your people; And there shall be a time of trouble, such as never was since there was a nation, even to that time. And at that time your people shall be delivered, every one who is found written in the book. And many of those who sleep in the dust of the earth shall awake, some to everlasting life, some to shame and everlasting contempt".*

Thus, the return of Jesus (Michael in this intepretation) will see the destruction of the king of the north, the establishment of the Kingdom and the resurrection, as many other prophecies clearly show.

An earlier time of the end

There has been another interpretation of these verses that readers might care to consider. The following suggestions could be regarded as an initial fulfilment and do not necessarily rule out a future application – dual fulfilments are a feature of many Bible prophecies.

As we have already seen, some suggest that the great king of verse 36 onward is Herod the Great, and that verse 40 onward continues the historical events that led up to Israel's "time of the end" in AD 70.

This alternative scenario suggested for the fulfilment of verses 40–45 follows on logically and historically from the accepted interpretation of verses 5–35, as outlined in *The Exposition of Daniel*.

As previously mentioned, a commonly held understanding is

that verse 40 suddenly jumps forward from a couple of hundred years BC (the universally accepted view of vv.34–35 being the Maccabean revolt) to the events at the return of Christ well over 2000 years later. The king of the north, which earlier in the chapter was clearly the ruler of the northern territory of Alexander's fragmented empire, is transformed into the invader of Ezekiel 38–39. This understanding is apparently confirmed by the following references to the resurrection in the opening of chapter 12 – obviously an end-times event.

Clearly there is a long gap to be placed *somewhere* in the concluding verses of chapter 11 and the early part of chapter 12, but are we correct in placing it between verses 39 and 40, or would it be more appropriate between later verses?

Kings of the north and south in the first century BC

If the additional view now being suggested is considered, then verses 36–39 could be seen as depicting events that immediately followed on from the Hasmonean rule. The rise of King Herod the Great with his bombastic utterances and authoritarian rule certainly fits the description of verse 36 – he indeed did "according to his will", as history shows. The other descriptions of this king could also be equated with the achievements and character of Herod, as mentioned earlier.

This suggests that this section of the prophecy really begins in verse 36, which describes the king that exalts himself. Previous verses immediately before verse 36 are widely accepted as referring to the time of Antiochus Epiphanes and the Maccabees. So it would seem logical to expect that the king of verse 36 onward is a ruler that immediately followed on from that time, and that this is the same person described later on in the chapter.

If "the king" of verse 36 is taken as a reference to Herod the Great, then a different scenario is envisaged, and one that culminates in the destruction of Jerusalem by the Romans in AD 70. In this case the "time of the end" refers to the end of the Jewish commonwealth.

Is there any link between the symbology of verses 11.40–12.1 and the actual events of the times of Herod and his successors?

The history of the period does show some remarkable features. Judea became a Roman province in 65 BC, and in 37 BC the young Herod was made king by Rome. At that time Rome was ruled by what is known as a triumvirate – consisting of Octavian (later known as Augustus), Marcus Aemilius Lepidus and Mark Antony. The old Ptolomaic kingdom in the south was ruled by Queen Cleopatra. Mark Antony fell out with Octavian and went to Egypt and allied himself to Cleopatra. Antony made a bid for total power, and Octavian responded by assembling a huge fleet of 400 ships to confront him: the "many ships" of verse 40. This resulted in the famous battle of Actium in 31 BC in which Antony and Cleopatra were defeated.

Following up on this victory, Augustus marched into Syria and down through Palestine into Egypt, which was still a wealthy country, but not into the Nabatean kingdoms on the site of ancient Ammon and Moab (v.41). Herod, ever the crafty diplomat, placated Augustus and retained his throne. History records that the Romans then spoiled Egypt's "treasures" and extended their conquest to Libya and Ethiopia. This is paralleled by the angel's account: *"He shall enter the countries, overwhelm them, and pass through. He shall also enter the Glorious Land, and many countries shall be overthrown; but these shall escape from his hand: Edom, Moab, and the prominent people of Ammon... and the land of Egypt will not escape."*

The similarity with the predictions is striking. In most versions the king of the south is described as attacking "the king" of the previous verse, that is, Herod. But Young's literal translation describes it as being "with" him. This fits the situation better, as Herod was originally Antony's confederate. The king of the south, Antony (supported at first by Herod), did "attack" Octavian, the king of the north, who then counter-attacked by sea and land as already described. Octavian responded by coming *"against him like a whirlwind, with chariots, horsemen and many ships"*, by which he "overwhelmed" them and entered the "Glorious Land", bypassing Edom, Moab and Ammon.

According to the interpretation outlined here, verses 44–45 revert to the actions of Herod (the antecedent of the "he" of verse 44 being seen as the "king" of vv.36–39). The troubling news from the east and north is the threat posed by information brought by the wise men. These originated in the east (but because of the intervening desert would have arrived in Jerusalem from the north) with news of the newly born King of Israel; resulting in Herod's "great fury" against the Bethlehem innocents.

Daniel also describes this king building palaces at Jerusalem, and then his lonely demise: *"And he shall plant the tents of his palace between the seas and the glorious holy mountain; yet he shall come to his end, and no one will help him"* (11.45). History records that Herod did in fact build two palaces in Jerusalem (between the Mediterranean and Dead seas) and also that he died a lonely and agonising death despite the efforts of his physicians.

At this juncture (and remember there are no chapter divisions in the original) Daniel is told that: *"Michael shall stand up, the great prince who stands watch over the sons of your people; and there shall be a time of trouble, such as never was since there was a nation, even to that time. And at that time your people shall be delivered, every one who is found written in the book. And many of those who sleep in the dust of the earth shall awake, some to everlasting life, some to shame and everlasting contempt"* (12.1–2).

Who is Michael?

It might be thought that this question is superfluous, because it is almost universally accepted that here is a reference to the returned Jesus. Even so, the scriptural identity of Michael is worth pursuing. We need to have full justification even for our long-standing beliefs.

First, the meaning of the name describes one "who is like God". Clearly this is appropriately used of Jesus, who was the manifestation of the Almighty: *"He that has seen me has seen the Father"* (John 14.9).

But others, notably the angels, have also demonstrated this principle, as the essential doctrine of God manifestation indicates. God said to Israel in the wilderness: *"Behold, I send an angel before you… Beware of him and obey His voice… for my name is in him"* (Exodus 23.20–21). There are several examples of angels bearing the Yahweh name and speaking as if they were God Himself, for example the angel that appeared to Abraham (Genesis 18.1,13). Another angel (or maybe the same one that oversaw the nation in the wilderness) appeared to Joshua, wielding a drawn sword as *"The commander of the LoR D's army"* (Joshua 5.15). Each of these was one "who is like God", because of the role God had entrusted to them.

This possibility that Michael could be an angel is strengthened by Jude's reference. Referring to the confrontation between the regathered Jews and their Samaritan opponents as described in Zechariah 3, the apostle speaks of *"Michael the archangel"* (v.9).

Coming to the prophecy of Daniel, there are two other references to Michael apart from that in chapter 12. The angel who was giving this last prophecy to Daniel (possibly Gabriel, 8.16; 9.21) refers to Michael as *"one of the chief princes"*, who came to help him, when he had been left alone with the kings of Persia (10.13).

This sharing of duties by Michael and his fellow angel is confirmed by the next reference: *"But I will tell you what is inscribed in the book of truth: there is none who contends by my side against these except Michael, your prince"* (RSV). It seems that these archangels were termed "princes", but Jesus is their superior, being termed in contrast "Prince of princes" in chapter 8.25.

So when we come to chapter 12.1, we are told the role of Michael: *"At that time Michael shall stand up, The great prince who stands watch over* [has charge of, RSV] *the sons of your people"*, what justification do we have for changing the identity of Michael from the angel that had charge of Daniel's people to that of Jesus?

Admittedly, if we accept that the conventional understanding of the time of the end prophecy is the only possibility, there is probably no alternative to believing that Michael is Jesus and that the "time of trouble" refers to the divine judgements poured out on a godless world.

An absolutely unique time of trouble

But that reference to the time of trouble itself raises a difficulty – it was to be without parallel ever since nations (or maybe the nation of Israel) had existed: *"And there shall be a time of trouble, such as **never was since there was a nation, even to that time**"* (Daniel 12.1). There is little escaping the meaning of these words – that time of trouble was to be completely unprecedented. Here it is interesting to note the words of Jesus concerning the AD 70 destruction of Jerusalem. Here he clearly refers to Daniel 12.1 and its unique time of trouble, but applies it to the destruction of Jerusalem by the Romans: *"For then there will be great tribulation, such as has not been since the beginning of the world until this time, **no, nor ever shall be**"* (Matthew 24.21).

These words of Jesus *"nor ever shall be"* present a problem if a fulfilment of Daniel 12.1 is yet future. Both Jesus and Daniel say that this time of trouble is absolutely unique. Until the end of time there will be no such trouble as is depicted in Daniel 12.1. Yet Jesus clearly applies it to the events of AD 70. It is suggested that this rules out a yet future time of trouble. Clearly, from other Scriptures we know that there will be much trouble at the return of Jesus, but it will not be so severe as in AD 70. Therefore, on this understanding, God's judgements on the world at Christ's return are different from the time of trouble depicted in Daniel 12.1.

Did the prophecy therefore predict to Daniel that at the end of Israel's national life Michael would stand up, not for blessing, but for punishment? The use of the word "stand" sometimes has the implication of judgement. Isaiah uses the same word translated "stand" when he says: *"The LORD stands up to plead, and stands to judge the people"* (Isaiah 3.13). Habakkuk had a vision where God *"stood, and shook the earth; he looked, and made the nations tremble"* (3.6 NIV). So it is possible that the AD 70 destruction of Jerusalem in punishment of the Jews for their murder of Jesus is here indicated and Michael, Israel's national angel, was to supervise the event.

Those written in the book delivered

But some would escape these judgements. In his Olivet prophecy Jesus seems to have these chapters in Daniel very much in mind when he predicted the destruction of Jerusalem. He told the disciples: *"So when you see the desolating sacrilege spoken of by the prophet Daniel, standing in the holy place (let the reader understand), then let those who are in Judea flee to the mountains"* (Matthew 24.15–16). And this is what happened to the faithful disciples when Jerusalem fell. They fled in safety to Pella, experiencing exactly what Daniel was told: *"At that time your people shall be delivered; every one who is found written in the book"* (12.1).

Where is the gap?

As mentioned previously, every interpretation of these closing verses of Daniel must acknowledge that somewhere between chapter 11.40 and the remaining verses of the prophecy there must be a gap where many intervening years are passed over. In the case of the conventional understanding, this occurs between 11.39 and 11.40, the prophecy's fulfilment jumping from the second century BC to the yet future invasion of Israel by the king of the north and the return of Jesus.

But what of the parallel suggestion outlined above that refers it to the events surrounding the AD 70 destruction of Jerusalem? It is suggested that here the gap comes between verse 1 and 2 of chapter 12. Having referred to the destruction of Jerusalem in that time of trouble and the deliverance of the faithful from the Roman armies, the angel goes immediately forward to the time of their resurrection and reward – alongside, of course, that of all other faithful ones.

This sudden transfer of thought is very common in Scripture, and there are innumerable examples in the Old Testament. Indeed, it is a feature our Lord's Olivet prophecy that had Daniel as its background. Having predicted the destruction of Jerusalem by the Roman eagles (Matthew 24.28) Jesus straightway goes forward to the time of his return: *"Immediately after the tribulation of those days... then will appear the sign of the Son of man in heaven, and then all the tribes of the earth will mourn, and they will see the Son of man coming on the clouds of heaven with power and great glory"* (vv.29–30).

It would seem, therefore, that this alternative understanding of the role of the kings of the north and south is worth considering.

As with all the attempted exposition of prophecy in this book this chapter especially is put forward with diffidence and the recognition of our own frailty of understanding. We also recognise that there may be other legitimate interpretations of the events predicted in Daniel 11.40–12.2 as well as the two we have outlined. But we hope that this study may stimulate others to examine this amazing section of Daniel's prophecy in the spirit of Matthew's injunction: *"whoever reads let him understand"* (Matthew 24.15).

Chapter 14 Times and seasons

So far we have reviewed most of the prophecies that we believe impinge on the time of the end. As we now bring this study to a conclusion, it is with some trepidation that we touch on the question that has exercised the minds of God's children down the ages, and we say with Daniel: *"How long shall it be to the end of these wonders?"* (Daniel 12.6 RSV)

There are general signs that indicate that in the early part of the twenty-first century we are truly living in the "last days": the restored nation of Israel being the most obvious one. But in addition, the Spirit has given us what appear to be more specific indications as to when Israel will be saved, and eventually the whole world receive the blessings of the Kingdom. Over the past 150 or more years these "time-periods" have been avidly studied, each generation often deriving comfort from an interpretation that suggested that the return of Jesus would occur within their lifetime. But the years have come and gone; and no doubt our Bible student forebears would have been astounded to be told that the events they looked for still awaited fulfilment in the twenty-first century.

But now, with the once-expected termination dates of almost all such prophecies behind us, there seems to be a feeling that there is not much point in studying them further. Indeed some suggest that these prophecies have little relevance to the time of the end, or that if they do their application is too obscure to be of much value. So, under cover of not knowing the "day or the hour" of Christ's return, some have put these prophecies to the back of their minds.

To us this seems a defeatist attitude that ignores several points. First, it seems inconceivable that detailed and specific time-periods would have been given if there were no possibility of their being of use. Second, there are now-completed similar periods that *have* proved accurate – the prophecy of the seventy weeks being an outstanding example; along with the exact rise and fall of the papacy as foretold in Revelation (see page 85).

So maybe it is time to look anew at these time-periods – especially those in Daniel. It might just be possible that some inherited preconceptions have prevented us from evaluating them aright. The following suggests some lines on which the prophecies can be re-examined.

A threatened globe

But first a general look at world conditions, which suggest that for the first time in its history the planet Earth is really reaching a crisis point. From several converging points of view the world as we know it is in a perilous state, with its future uncertain, humanly speaking. Probably the major concern at present is global warming. International symposia on the topic have concluded that if current temperature rises are maintained, then within comparatively few decades the whole earth could be severely compromised. They report that the polar ice has melted at an unprecedented rate, and the Arctic ice sheet could even disappear. The resultant flooding would submerge many of the major cities of the world. If climatic trends continue unabated, global warming will threaten our health, our cities, our farms and forests, beaches and wetlands, and other natural habitats.

If these forecasts are correct, our planet is now facing a potential catastrophe not even envisaged by previous generations. We suggest that this unique prospect could be an indication that we really are living in the last times. Unless divine intervention occurs soon, dire consequences may well occur.

Daniel's time-periods

These have been the study of Bible students over many years and, because they are numerically defined and seem to have an identifiable beginning and ending, have generated much interest and expectation. This of itself has brought encouragement and comfort, even if disappointment when the anticipated development has not taken place.

All Daniel's time-periods relate to Israel, and many have particular reference to the "sanctuary" – doubtless a reference to the temple site at Jerusalem.

The 2300 years

This is the first specific time-period revealed to Daniel, at the end of the vision of the ram (Persia) and the he goat (Greece): *"Then I heard a holy one speaking; and another holy one said to that certain one who was speaking, 'How long will the vision be, concerning the daily sacrifices and the transgression of desolation, the giving of both the sanctuary and the host to be trampled underfoot?' And he said to me, 'For two thousand three hundred days; then the sanctuary shall be cleansed'"* (Daniel 8.13–14). That this cleansing of the sanctuary was a long way ahead is indicated first by Daniel's symbolic death and resurrection (v.18), and then by the express statements of the angel: *"The vision is for the time of the end"* (v.17 RSV) and: *"The vision ... shall be for many days"* (v.26).

In passing, it should perhaps be mentioned that some (but not all) Septuagint versions give the length of the period as 2400 years, and this figure was accepted by John Thomas. But it now seems generally accepted that this is not the correct reading; an error being made in printing the Vatican edition of 1586, and since perpetuated.

The "little horn" of the goat

The immediate context of the statement concerning the 2300 days is that a "little horn" arose from one of the four horns of the goat. The goat represents the Greek Empire, and its four horns denote that Empire's division on the death of Alexander the Great. The little horn that emerged from one of these represents the Roman Empire that was eventually to defile the Jewish sanctuary and magnify itself against the prince of the host (v.11). The Romans did both in the first century AD when they crucified Jesus, and later, in AD 70, razed Jerusalem and destroyed *"the mighty and the holy people"* (v.24).

Assuming, on the "day for a year" principle, that a period of 2300 years is being predicted for the supremacy of this "little horn", we need to have starting and finishing points. The prophecy clearly terminates after Christ's return, when the sanctuary is "cleansed" after previously being "trodden under foot". Over the years, many starting points have been suggested, ranging from the destruction of Jerusalem by Nebuchadnezzar to the date when the prophecy was given to Daniel. This latter view was warmly taken up as a basic doctrine by the early Seventh Day Adventist movement, who confidently expected Jesus to return at the end of the 2300 years in 1844. When this did not occur they suffered what they called the "great disappointment", resulting in the loss of many members. This shows the danger of basing fundamental teaching on human interpretation of such prophecies. But the current Muslim presence on Jerusalem's temple platform clearly suggests that the 2300 years have not yet expired.

The power of Rome

At the risk of being accused of doing what previous would-be expositors have done, that is, fitting fulfilment of prophecy into one's own era – dare we make another suggestion? Do the 2300 years relate to the length of activity of the "little horn"? That clearly represents the Roman power which, in its various phases, was to continue until destroyed at the return of Christ (Daniel 8.25). Although the original Roman Empire has passed away, in other ways it has continued in various political and religious guises unto this day. Thus, the little horn parallels Daniel's fourth beast, which, he was told, would continue until being replaced by the Kingdom of God (Daniel 7.27). These various phases of the Roman influence and power are also depicted by the various beasts of Revelation, as described in chapter 11. So, should we not commence the 2300 years from the emergence of the power of Rome? When was this?

The new power – Rome

For many centuries Rome was simply the head of a city-state, but in the third century BC it expanded to include the whole of Italy. The actual year when this unification was completed is not completely clear, but most historians place it around 266 BC, others at 261BC. Certainly, by the start of the first Punic war against Carthage in 263 BC the power of the united kingdom of Rome was being felt beyond the confines of Italy. The *Encyclopaedia Britannica* says of these years: "Italy had hitherto played no active part in Mediterranean politics, but, now that she was for the first time united, it was felt throughout the Mediterranean world that *a new power had arisen*" (14th edition, vol. 19, p.484, our italics).

It would seem reasonable, therefore, to date the commencement of the 2300 years at the "coming forth" of the little horn power at around 266–261 BC. Adding the 2300 years suggests that this power, in its various phases, would therefore continue until about AD 2034–2039, and then the sanctuary will finally be cleansed of all traces of its presence. Although at the time of writing this may seem quite distant, we have seen in previous studies that there is much activity foretold for the years immediately preceding the final destruction of Rome's successor – the "beast" that we have identified in earlier pages.

The 1290 and 1335 days

Right at the end of Daniel's ministry three other time-periods were revealed to him. The first, in response to the question: *"How long shall it be till the end of these wonders?"* (12.6 RSV) a period of *"a time, times, and half a time"* was given (v.7), after which the shattering of Israel's power will come to an end. We have already suggested a meaning for this on page 53.

In response to his later question: *"My Lord, what shall be the end of these things?"* Daniel was told that: *"The words are closed up and sealed till the time of the end"* (12.8–9). The divine messenger then indicated when that time of the end would be: *"And from the time that the daily sacrifice is taken away, and the abomination of desolation set up, there shall be one thousand two hundred and ninety days. Blessed is he that waits, and comes to the thousand three hundred and thirty-five days"* (vv.11–12). As with the 2300 years, at least one of these time-periods clearly terminates at events surrounding the establishment of the Kingdom, for Daniel was told: *"But you, go your way till the end: for you shall rest, and arise to your inheritance at the end of the days"* (v.13).

Over the years many and varied suggestions have been made as to how the 1290 days/years relate to historical events, and what the extra 45 years signify. In every one of these suggestions the assumption has been made that the starting point of both periods is the same, with most believing that the extra 45 years represents the time between the return of Jesus and the final establishment of the worldwide Kingdom of God.

Because of the much shorter period of time involved, most expositors have in some way equated the setting up of the "abomination that makes desolate" (RSV) with the rise of the Islamic power. Even so, most of the suggested end points of the prophecy have already expired.

Parallel or sequential?

But suppose we regard the two periods as sequential rather than running in parallel? We then have a total period of 2625 years (1290 + 1335), with a significant event occurring after 1290 of those years had passed, leaving a further 1335 before the final fulfilment.

In terms of the prophecy the division between the two periods is as follows:

Part 1: *"The daily sacrifice is taken away, and the abomination of desolation set up, there shall be one thousand two hundred and ninety days".*

Part 2: *"The one thousand three hundred and thirty-five days"* with its subsequent blessing.

Taking away the daily sacrifice

The taking away of the daily temple sacrifice and the setting up of the abomination (Part 1) do not necessarily describe the same event. One event could mark the *beginning* and the other the *end* of the 1290-year period. Young's literal translation suggests that this might be so, making the latter phrase read: *"... and to the time of the giving out of the desolating abomination..."*. If this understanding is correct, then there are two separate events that need historical identification – the removal of the daily sacrifice, followed much later by the setting up of the abomination.

For Daniel, a captive in Babylon, the reference to the daily sacrifice in the temple being taken away would undoubtedly take his mind back to campaigns of Nebuchadnezzar against Jerusalem. There were three of these, culminating in the destruction of the city and sanctuary. The first occurred in 606 BC, when Daniel was taken captive in the third year of Jehoiakim (Daniel 1.1). Eight years later, in 598 BC, the main campaign took place, when King Jehoiachin and ten thousand of the cream of Judah were taken captive. The temple was plundered and its treasures taken to Babylon (2 Kings 24.10–16). The *"poorest people of the land"* remained and, after being ruled by the traitorous Zedekiah, were finally either taken captive or killed in the third campaign, when their city and temple were destroyed in 586 BC.

There is no actual mention of any disruption of temple services following the Babylonians' first attack in 606 BC – although for Daniel himself the daily sacrifice indeed ceased, and the temple vessels were taken to Babylon (Daniel 1.2), thus disrupting the temple routines. The 598 BC campaign would certainly have had an effect on the temple services, although there is no actual record of cessation of the daily sacrifice. But we learn from Ezekiel, who lived in Babylon whilst the "bad figs" (Jeremiah 24) continued in Jerusalem under Zedekiah, that until the final captivity the temple worship was profaned by idolatry, sun worship and other heathen practices (Ezekiel 8–11). So it is possible that the daily sacrifice was discontinued with the exile of Jehoiachin. But if not, then all such sacrifices certainly ceased on the final destruction of the temple in 586 BC.

So it would seem that 606, 598 or 586 BC could be the commencement of the 1290 years, and ending AD 684, 692 and 704 respectively. See author's note on p.134

After 1290 years, the "abomination" set up

Adding 1290 years to these dates brings us well into the Mohammedan era, when the Caliphs ruled Jerusalem. After desecrating the temple platform – even to the extent of using the once holy site as a manure heap – those rulers built a shrine over the rock that once had been the place of the ark of the covenant. This rock also became sacred to Islam, as it was believed that it was from there that Mohammed ascended to heaven. This shrine – the Dome of the Rock – was commenced in AD 684 and completed about AD 692 and still exists today as the dominant feature of the platform. The year AD 684, when the building of the "abomination of desolation" commenced, is exactly 1290 years from Nebuchadnezzar's first attack on Jerusalem in 606 BC.

Adding 1290 years to the time of the second attack on Jerusalem, 598 BC, brings us to AD 692, when the construction of the Dome was completed.

If we take the 586 BC complete destruction of Jerusalem as the starting point another possible ending of the 1290 is reached. At the south end of the temple platform in Jerusalem is another holy Muslim site: the El-Aksa Mosque. This, unlike the Dome, is a place of worship. It was originally built as a wooden structure and rebuilt in stone a few years after the Dome was completed. The date of the "setting up" of this building is variously given as AD 704 or 709, possibly indicating the time involved. And if we come forward 1290 years from Nebuchadnezzar's complete destruction of Israel's sanctuary in 586 BC, we arrive at AD 704, the very time the permanent El-Aksa Mosque was being built.

So, by adding the 1290 years to any of the three possible dates of the cessation of the daily sacrifice by Nebuchadnezzar we come to the reign of the desolating power in Jerusalem and the very time when the "abominations" were being set up on the site of Israel's sanctuary. This seems to suggest that we are on the right lines.

1335 years and the "end of the days"

We now add to these dates the 1335 years to arrive at the "end of the days" (Daniel 12.13), looking at each one in turn. If the above reasoning is correct, then at least one of the following dates refers to the final purification of the place that once held the divine sanctuary.

If the 1290 years began at Nebuchadnezzar's first invasion in 606 BC and terminated at the commencement of building the Dome of the Rock in AD 684, adding 1335 years brings us to the year **2019**. See author's note on p.134

If the 1290 years began in 598 BC with Nebuchadnezzar's second invasion and ended with the completion of the Dome of the Rock in AD 692, then the end of the 1335 years, with its ultimate blessing, would be in the year **2027**.

If Nebuchadnezzar's complete destruction of the temple is used as the starting point of the 1290, then the end of the 1335 and the cleansing of the sanctuary would be in **2039**. This is very similar to the 2034–2039 date arrived at in our understanding of the prophecy of the 2300 days/years of Daniel 8.14: the time when *"the sanctuary shall be cleansed"*.

That all these suggested termination dates are within a few years of each other seems to indicate that this interpretation of the 1290 and 1335 days is worthy of consideration. The variation in the completion dates suggests the possibility (and it is only put forward as that) that these differing dates mark different stages in the time of the end programme. It could be that for Daniel himself (appropriately, as the one taken captive in 606 BC is being addressed by the angel) the "end of the days" will be the first of these alternative dates, 2019, when he shall "arise" to his inheritance (Daniel 12.13). If so, the resurrection is near indeed.

The other endings of the 1335 years, 2027 or 2039, could mark the final cleansing of the sanctuary after the world nations have been completely subdued.

An extensive programme

If these dates are relevant, then the years leading up to the final purification of the site of Israel's former sanctuary should see much divine activity. In the period from the present until the "end of the days" will be the attack on Israel by the northern invaders, the return of Jesus, the judgement and reward of the saints, the establishment of the nucleus of the Kingdom in Jerusalem, and the preaching of the "ever-lasting gospel". This will be followed by the refusal of many nations to submit to Christ, then their gathering together in an attempt to unseat him, resulting in defeat at the battle of Armageddon. Only then will the "little horn" or "beast" power be destroyed and the land finally cleansed. Indeed, John Thomas and many earlier Bible students believed that it would take forty years to effect this transition between the kingdom of men and the Kingdom of God.

So we must remember that these suggested dates would mark the very final stages of the time of the end programme. As we believe that the actual return of Jesus to his brethren and sisters will be fairly early on in this sequence, that event could be quite soon. The exhortation of Jesus is still very appropriate: *"When these things begin to happen, look up, and lift up your heads; for your redemption draws near"* (Luke 21.28).

Readers will have to decide for themselves the reasonable-ness of the suggestions put forward in these last two chapters. We believe that, in view of the failure of previous interpretations, they deserve some consideration. We also recognise that these prophecies may contain a dual fulfilment, and that there could be secondary applications to other past periods of Israel's history.

Another indication?

In addition to the time-periods of Daniel, there is another possible hint as to the timing of the end days. It relates to the events of the crossing of the Jordan as described in the book of Joshua.

Israel, having left the wilderness where they had been sustained by the manna, was about to cross the Jordan – a river that descended from a place called Adam (Joshua 3.16) and terminated in the sterile waters of the Dead Sea. The entry into the Promised Land was made possible by the ark of the covenant going ahead and causing the obstructing river to be dried up, enabling the Israelites to cross.

All the events relating to the exodus are clearly typical of the redemption of the true Israel of God, and this is no exception. The Jordan flowing from Adam to the Dead Sea is a fitting emblem of the downward path that all mankind has taken since Eden. But after being in the wilderness and sustained spiritually only by God's Word, God's people, by means of the symbolic Christ-ark, breach the downward progress to death experienced by all who have descended from Adam, and cross into the Kingdom of God.

Two thousand cubits

With this in mind, we ask if there is any significance in the prescribed distance between the ark and the following Israelites. Joshua was told: *"Yet there shall be a space between you and it, about two thousand cubits by measure: come not near unto it, that you may know the way by which you must go: for you have not passed this way heretofore"* (v.4 KJV). Why this specified distance? Could it be that it represents the interval between the first and second crossings of the symbolic Jordan? Christ, after his resurrection, was the first to enter into immortality, and he will be followed by the redeemed saints after an interval indicated by the 2000 cubits.

If so, representing the 2000 cubits as 2000 years gives an interesting parallel. Most scholars believe that Jesus was born between 7 and 4 BC, thus his crucifixion and subsequent glorification would be between AD 27 and 30. Add "about" 2000 years to this and we arrive at about the same era for the setting up of the Kingdom as we have deduced from the Daniel time-periods, that is, around 2030.

Final thoughts

Over my lifetime there have been many dramatic international events that have heightened a belief that the coming of Jesus was then close at hand. Older readers will remember the Israeli war of independence, the Suez crisis of 1956, the Six Day War of 1967 in which Jerusalem was freed from Gentile domination, the Yom Kippur war in 1973 – each of which in turn heightened the anticipation that the return of Jesus was imminent. But each crisis passed and expectations were disappointed. And at intervals such crises have come and gone up to the present day. This need not disturb us, but should make us patient.

We like to compare these events with the incoming tide. Most of us will have watched the waves rolling up a beach, and seen the waters gradually approaching the high tide mark. A big wave comes far up the beach and we may think that this must be the one that will reach the highest point. But it recedes, only to be followed by another, and then another. Each one recedes and the expectation subsides. But all the time the sea is inexorably encroaching and we know that one of these big waves will mark the climax.

So it is that even today there occur political crises that excite expectations, followed by an apparent return to near normality. But we must not be discouraged, for all the time the "high tide" is coming nearer, and at last one of these "waves" will herald the event that signals the return of Christ.

*****

In bringing to an end this study of the prophecies relating to the time of the end we stress that the main objective has been to help us be aware of the signs of the times and the need for personal preparation. Whatever the validity of all the foregoing, the fact remains that whenever Christ returns to his saints, it will still come to them as a surprise: *"Behold, I come as a thief"*. Hence his next comment, which all do well to heed: *"Blessed is he who watches…"* (Revelation 16.15).

Author's note: The dates determined by adding a time period to a BC start date should be increased by one if the stated end date is AD because there is no year zero. That means that (e.g.) the calculated "end of days" would be in the period 2020-2028, not 2019-2027 (see pp 128 and 130).

Scripture Reference Index